The BEST MOMENT of YOUR LIFE

100 LIFE-CHANGING TRAVEL EXPERIENCES

FOREWORD

What is the best moment of your life? It's a simple question to ask, a much harder one to answer. I should know. Over the past year I've asked it of hundreds of people who've travelled the globe, and often had to wait patiently for the answer. But every response – judiciously plucked from a lifetime's worth of memorable moments – was always worth the wait.

Needless to say, the quality of replies made selecting the top 100 responses to fill this title a very difficult prospect indeed. What I hope to convey with the stories that I have chosen is the sheer variety of ways that travel can positively affect your life. Like the lives we live, each of these experiences is unique, both in how it plays out and how it has affected the author afterwards ('The Take Away').

For some, the best moment couldn't be more important, literally separating their life into a before and an after. This was certainly the case for me, as my life was transformed during my first foray into India (p. 8). There, on the bank of the River Ganges, I realised the biggest tragedy of my life wouldn't be dying – it would be not actually living. Another of the lives divided distinctly in two is that of actor, director and writer Andrew McCarthy. Although walking the Camino de Santiago in northern Spain (p. 36), he wasn't expecting his moment, yet it crept up on him regardless. And rather than being marked with joy and laughter, it was framed with tears and sorrow. Interestingly, its significance was actually lost on him at the time and was only to be discovered the following morning.

Other moments clearly mark high points or adventurous accomplishments in the lives of those who have lived them, whether summiting Yosemite's Half Dome (p. 60), cycling 11,000km around the shores of the Mediterranean (p. 80) or proving to yourself that parenthood won't curb your adventurous spirit (p. 84). For Katalin Thomann in Tibet, it was as simple as finding true love (p. 42).

Family bonds are key to most of our lives, so it's not surprising that they can play a role in some of our greatest moments. For Cristian Bonetto, it was travelling with his mother to her childhood haunt of Alexandria, Egypt – he not only witnessed elements of the city first that he'd heard countless stories of, but more importantly he discovered another wonderful side to the woman who raised him (p. 12).

Wading into your own history or that of others is a remarkable thing, and it can certainly cement a moment's importance in your life. This could be playing a part of history itself, such Duff Battye witnessing the first free speech of Nelson Mandela (p. 22), or it may be seemingly travelling back in time to touch a forgotten past. Emma Thomson's explorations of Sudan's pyramids at Begrawiya was a moving example of the latter (p. 90).

The power and majesty of wildlife, whether a captivating encounter with a mountain gorilla (p. 62), a fleeting glimpse of a snow leopard (p. 208) or long-awaited tiger sighting (p. 92), is also something that clearly impacts the lives of those who have witnessed it. The beauty and sheer scale of our environment that houses all of Earth's creatures has proved to be no less influential in travellers' lives, with best moments sparked by everything from the endless cosmos and dramatic deserts to twinkling city skylines and calving glaciers. The larger the backdrop, the more we seem to be able to bring some perspective to our place on this planet. As Adrian Phillips (p. 194) puts it so brilliantly: 'Strange as it sounds, nothing is more liberating – exhilarating even – than to experience a true sense of insignificance.'

Lastly, it's the interactions with our fellow humans that often spark moments of a lifetime. Opening yourself up to others, even at the expense of the best-laid plans, can often provide rewards you never dreamed possible. As my father says, 'Being present is a present.'

Matt Phillips

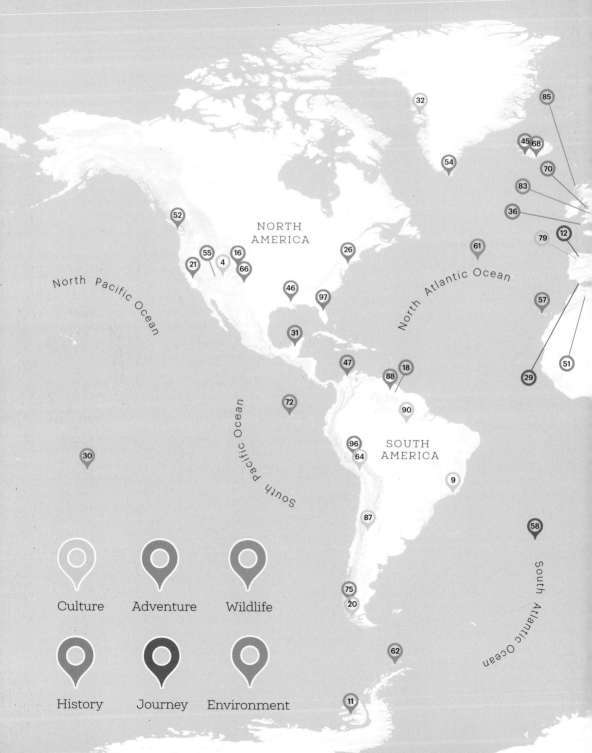

NORTH AMERICA

North Pacific Ocean

South Pacific Ocean

North Atlantic Ocean

SOUTH AMERICA

South Atlantic Ocean

Culture

Adventure

Wildlife

History

Journey

Environment

CONTENTS

1 Discovering Life on the Bank of the Ganges
Matt Phillips *8*

2 An Egyptian Homecoming
Cristian Bonetto *12*

3 Ice Skating on a Glass Lake
Duncan Craig *14*

4 Navajo Ceremony: Opening the Door
Aaron Millar *16*

5 Finding Life on the Tour du Mont Blanc
Ian MacEacheran *18*

6 Witnessing Mandela's First Free Speech Duff Battye *22*

7 Bewitched by Lions
Korina Miller *24*

8 Touching History at the Western Wall Anita Isalska *26*

9 Carnival's Wave of *Alegría*
Robert Landon *28*

10 Stories of the Trans-Siberian Railway John Lee *32*

11 Shooting Star Below the Antarctic Circle
Jurriaan Teulings *34*

12 Putting Fear to Bed on the Camino Andrew McCarthy *36*

13 Passing the Flinch Test
Brian Jackman *40*

14 Love, Light and Trekking in Tibet Katalin Thomann *42*

15 Encountering Kuchi Nomads Paul Clammer *44*

16 Cliff Camping in Colorado
Jonathan Thompson *46*

17 Pacific Perspective
Simon Heptinstall *50*

18 Retracing the Slave Revolt
John Gimlette *52*

19 First Watch on the Coral Sea Ruth Cosgrove *54*

20 On Horseback with Gauchos Brett Atkinson *56*

21 Climbing Half Dome
Neil Wilson *60*

22 An Enlightening Encounter with Mountain Gorillas
Jane Powell *62*

23 Rousing Respect
William Allen *64*

24 Temples at Dawn
Nicky Holford *66*

25 Coral Island Castaway
William Gray *70*

26 Central Park Stroll in the Snow
Tasmin Waby *72*

27 Remote Mountain Rescue
Stephen Lioy *74*

28 In the Arabian Sands
Oliver Smith *76*

29 Bicyling Beyond Fear
Ethan Gelber *80*

30 Swimming with Whales
Jean-Bernard Carillet *82*

31 Pre-Parenthood Pyramid
Liz Edwards *84*

32 An Arctic Picnic
Nigel Tisdall *86*

33 Dunes, Glyphs and Pyramids Emma Thomson *90*

34 Long-Awaited Tiger Sighting Daniel McCrohan *92*

35 Post-Tsunami Volunteering
Stephen Phelan *94*

36 Coast Path Conquest
Paul Bloomfield *96*

37 Riding the Midnight Train
Wailana Kalama *100*

38 Floating Among Giants on Canoe Safari
Aurelia India Birwood *102*

39 Hitting New Himalayan Highs Stephanie Pearson *104*

40 Petra by Candlelight
Mike MacEacheran *106*

41 A Brotherhood on Kili
David Gorvett *110*

42 Staring into an Active Volcano
James Gabriel Martin *112*

43 Cycling the Temple Trail
Joe Minihani *114*

44 Good Heavens Above
Sally Gray *116*

45 Journey to the Centre of the Earth Chris Zeiher *120*

46 Following Finn on the Mississippi Nicola Trup *122*

47 Exploring Colombia's 'Lost' City Sarah Reid *124*

48 Exploring Precious Madagascan Forests
Emma Gregg *126*

49 Lightening the Load
Ashley Garver *130*

50 Discovering Ancient Persia
Claire Beyer *132*

51 The Paris Opera in the Desert Brendan Sainsbury *134*

52 Finding Perspective on the West Coast Trail
Dayna Aamodt *136*

53 Death and Reincarnation on the Kora Tony Wheeler *140*

54 Jetty of Joy Richard Mellor *142*

55 Forgetting Solitude in the Grand Canyon Amy C Balfour *144*

56 Taking the Plunge with Whale Sharks Georgina Wilson-Powell *146*

57 Topping El Teide Paul Stiles *150*

58 Oceanic Odyssey Lucy Corne *152*

59 Looking Up to the Wonder of Penny Carroll *154*

60 Emerging from the Gobi Desert Benedict Allen *156*

61 Sperm Whales Gathering Sarah Outen *160*

62 A Window into Antarctica Jamie Lafferty *162*

63 A Writer's Vision Anthony Ham *164*

64 It's Not About the Bucket List Mike Howard *166*

65 Snowed-Out on Wutai Shan Damian Harper *170*

66 Soul Food on Mt Bierstadt Laura Brown *172*

67 Touching Tibet Antonia Bolingbroke-Kent *174*

68 A String of Black Pearls Sophie Cunningham *178*

69 Flying Flip-Flops and the Birkenstock Thomas Mills *180*

70 Wild Camping in Wales Phoebe Smith *182*

71 Tracking Desert Elephants Simon Parker *184*

72 Watching Lava Flow Oliver Berry *188*

73 Biking (and Bagging) Mont Ventoux Lori Rackl *190*

74 Lost (and Found) without Language or Direction Fionn Davenport *192*

75 Road-Tripping on the Carretera Austral Adrian Phillips *194*

76 Epiphany at Notre Dame Don George *198*

77 Summiting Mt Elbrus Hugo Turner *200*

78 Chasing the Northern Lights Nick Boulos *202*

79 Golden City Mornings Kait Reynolds *206*

80 Tracking Snow Leopards Mike Unwin *208*

81 The Great Hindu Gathering Mark Stratton *212*

82 Eyes Over the Outback Ross Turner *216*

83 Unlikely Encounter on the Thames Marcel Theroux *218*

84 Follow Me: Japanese Hospitality Katharine Nelson *220*

85 Carefree Campervan Adventure Hannah Summers *222*

86 The Ultima Thule Everest Expedition Art Wolfe *226*

87 Learning to Love Solitude Abigail Butcher *228*

88 Guyana's Greatest Gift Chris Leadbeater *230*

89 Face to Face with Seven Lions Mark Eveleigh *232*

90 Life Lessons in the Amazon Anne Howard *236*

91 A Mountain Gazelle Suzanne Joinson *238*

92 A True Transition in Transit Pico Iyer *240*

93 Skiiing Up, Snowboarding Down Toby Skinner *242*

94 A Free Ride - Gary Arndt *246*

95 Twilight Surf Duncan Madden *248*

96 Moment at Machu Picchu Susan Kurosawa *250*

97 Space Shuttle Launch Paul Brady *252*

98 Meeting the Naga Babas Gopi Kallayil *256*

99 Riding the Road of Bones Charley Boorman *258*

100 Making a Connection Laura Millar *260*

1

A sadhu rows a boat along the Ganges in Varanasi

DISCOVERING LIFE ON THE BANK OF THE GANGES

VARANASI, INDIA

Below: space is at a premium as Hindus gather on the steps of the Ganges

I was about to travel alone for the first time in my life, and – not to sound overly melodramatic – I didn't think I was going to make it home. India was calling, and on my back was a bag half-full of 300 hypodermic needles. I'd just learned a couple weeks earlier that every 12 hours, like clockwork, I'd need to pull one out and inject myself in the stomach with blood thinner. Despite my overwhelming fear of death, I still knew I needed to go – I was a successful young geologist but wasn't happy with life, and I hoped this solo adventure would be the kick in the backside my soul needed.

I landed in Varanasi, arguably the most overwhelming city in India. It's a particularly sacred place for Hindus to die (liberating them from the cycle of birth, death and reincarnation), so the city welcomes countless Indian pilgrims who are nearing the end of their days. The sight of corpses is commonplace, and the first of many was carried past me within minutes of arrival. The streets were also heaving with life and poverty, and all the sights, sounds and smells that come along with it. The intensity of the situation was beyond anything that I had ever imagined, let alone experienced. Yet when I reached the western bank of the River Ganges, and looked down over all the funeral pyres to the grass-covered floodplains on the opposite bank, I felt such a sense of peace and calm.

By Matt Phillips

Pilgrims bathe in
the river to wash
away their sins

The Take Away

On the bank of the Ganges I witnessed
life and death on full display, and at that
moment I knew I'd not only love India, but
my life too. My biggest realisation? The
biggest tragedy wouldn't be dying – it would
be not actually living. I was right. That scared
young geologist didn't return home. I did.

The Build Up

Varanasi is one of the world's oldest
continually inhabited cities, and is believed
to date back to the 12th century BC.
Though it wasn't until almost two millennia
later that its importance rose when the
Indian theologian Shankaracharya unified
the currents of thought in Hinduism.

Funeral pyres have existed here for
thousands of years, and they burn non-stop.

But pilgrims don't just come here to die and
be cremated at Manikarnika Ghat, they also
visit to wash away their sins in the waters of
the Ganges and to worship the river itself.

The most moving times to visit the
Ganges are at dawn, when the river
and *ghats* (series of steps leading down
to the water) are glowing in the day's
first rays of light, and at sunset when
ganga aarti occurs at Dashashwamedh
Ghat. The latter ritual involves fire being
offered to the Goddess Ganga – you'll
see countless *diya* (clay dishes), each
bearing flowers and a candle, placed
in the river. The sight of these glowing
tributes floating down a blackened
Ganges in the dark is truly astounding.

Varanasi is well connected to the
rest of India by train, bus and plane.

2

AN EGYPTIAN HOMECOMING

ALEXANDRIA, EGYPT

As an Australian kid filled with wanderlust, I would devour tales of my Italian mother's childhood in Alexandria, Egypt, a city she left due to political unrest in 1967. Her Mediterranean memories were filled with multiple languages and horse-drawn carriage rides to Montaza Palace. Many life chapters later, we visited her 'beato Egitto' (blessed Egypt) together. I remember staring out the dusty train window at Alexandria's softly crumbling Belle Époque buildings, pondering the images racing through my mother's mind: my lithe, quiet nonno (grandfather) arriving home with trays of French pastries, teenage crushes on Sidi Bishr beach. Curiously, this was also my own homecoming. Although I had never physically been to Alexandria, I had long ridden its retro trams and walked its seafront Corniche in my imagination.

The following days were a whirlwind of reunions and anecdotes. Though the city had changed – fewer miniskirts, more hijabs, the construction of the spectacular Bibliotheca Alexandrina – traces of my mother's Alexandria remained: antique stores filled with the wealth of long-gone expats, the faded grandeur of the Trianon patisserie, the harmonious blend of Islamic and European architecture. Its cosmopolitan pedigree also lived on in the faded elegance of my mother's friend's living room. Under an heirloom chandelier they caught up on 37 years of gossip,

swinging effortlessly between Italian, French, English and Arabic, sipping mint tea and scrutinising photographs. I will never forget the radiant glow of a woman who had finally reconnected with her past, her hometown. 'We're here, Mum. We made it.'

By Cristian Bonetto

The Take Away

This trip will always epitomise the power of travel to better understand yourself, your loved ones and your history. Just like migrants and their offspring, Alexandria has been shaped by many cultures and influences. The result is a fluid, sometimes contradictory sense of self that speaks deeply to me.

The Build Up

Alexandria's international gateway is Burg Al Arab Airport, located about 45km southwest of the city. Most flights connect Alexandria to the Arabian Peninsula as well as North African destinations. Cairo Airport services significantly more airlines and routes, with non-stop flights to and from Europe, North America and Asia. Direct trains to Alexandria (LE70-100) run several times daily from Cairo's Ramses Station, with a journey time of around two and a half hours. Alexandria

local and Egyptologist Tamer Zakaria offers highly recommended English-language tours of the city; book tours in advance by email (tamerzakaria@yahoo.com).

To get around the city, your best bet is by taxi; working meters are next to non-existent, so it's best to negotiate a fare before starting your journey. There are also public transport options: informal microbuses that whizz along the Corniche, but as they don't have set stops you'll just have to shout your destination and they'll stop if going your way; buses, which you won't find particularly efficient; and a painfully slow tram with a bit of a fun factor. The best time to visit Alexandria is in either the spring or the autumn. Both seasons are also ideal times to visit the rest of the country.

Above: a sphinx standing guard at the Roman Pompey's Pillar in Alexandria
Left: Montazah Palace Lighthouse on the city's Mediterranean shoreline

3

ICE SKATING ON A GLASS LAKE

LAKE VÄTTERN, SWEDEN

'You'll feel like you're flying,' the excitable guide had told me over a bottle of something potent and Swedish the previous evening. I'd hidden my cynicism with a smile. I wasn't even sure what I was doing here, to be frank. Ice skating? Wasn't that all sequins and Bolero, mulled wine and festive mayhem?

No, as it turned out. The following morning found me racing across a lake surface so flawless that merely stepping out onto it had taken a giant leap of faith. Some 10m below, bathed in bright winter sunshine, every pebble and reed of the lake-bed zipped by in spectacular high definition.

They call this 'glass ice', an ephemeral phenomenon born of perfect water clarity and ideal conditions. For outdoor skaters, it's as good as it gets – Centre Court, on the opening day of Wimbledon. Our group of beginners had found it on Lake Vättern, the biggest of Sweden's estimated 100,000 lakes, and we weren't about to waste it.

A few inexpert chops at the pristine surface with my blade-fitted boots and I was racing once more (the speed-to-effort ratio is pleasingly skewed). I sucked in lungfuls of frosty, supercharged air and took in the epic vista of vast, sparkling lake fringed by snow-dusted forest. With my group duckling-ing far behind, there was nothing to interrupt either progress or train of thought; the only sound, an occasional bullwhip reverberation of a fresh crack in the ice reminding me that – despite what all my senses were telling me – I wasn't, in fact, flying.

By Duncan Craig
Assistant Travel Editor, The Sunday Times

You won't have as much fun if you forget these!

Top glass: *perfect ice conditions for Swedish skaters*

Sweden has some 1000 lakes to choose from

The Take Away

The experience opened my eyes to the sheer immensity of nature's playground and how our contrived imitations pale by comparison; festive ice rinks will certainly never be the same again. And it demonstrated our Scandinavian cousins' refreshingly grown-up approach to risk vs reward, embracing that increasingly outdated concept – personal responsibility.

The Build Up

Skating on natural ice trips in eastern Sweden are available through Nature Travels (naturetravels.co.uk) between January and March. Two levels are offered: Novice, for those who have rink skated or roller-bladed before and are able to skate without support; and Experienced, for those who are comfortable travelling longer distances. Both are guided and have a minimum age requirement of 16. Exact locations vary depending on ice conditions, with distances covered matched to the ability of the group. Hostel accommodation is provided, along with all equipment including skates, knee and elbow pads, poles and safety kit. A good level of fitness is required.

Other countries where tour skating, or wild skating, is common in the winter months include Finland, Austria and particularly the Netherlands, whose spontaneously organised, weather-dependent Elfstedentocht race – a circular route of almost 200km (125 miles) linking 11 northern cities – attracts tens of thousands of skaters. Outdoor skating is also found in various spots in North America, including the New England states of Vermont and New Hampshire (the latter's Lake Sunapee is particularly popular) and over the border in Canada. The Rideau Canal, which runs through the centre of Ottawa, becomes a 7.8km (4.8 mile) skateway in winter, dubbed the world's largest ice rink, with skates for hire (ottawatourism.com).

4

NAVAJO CEREMONY: OPENING THE DOOR

MONUMENT VALLEY NAVAJO NATION TRIBAL PARK, UTAH, USA

The medicine man stared through a crystal at a fire of hot coals that was spread out on the compacted red earth floor of his hogan, the traditional home of the Navajo. 'The fire is like an X-ray machine,' he said, placing a shiny black arrowhead in my left hand and fanning me with golden eagle feathers.

'I see your life reflected inside,' he continued. Then he began to chant low, guttural sounds in his native tongue – rhythmic words, like a drum beat, wavering with emotion as he called to the Holy Spirits to come down and bless our fire.

'Why are you here?' he said suddenly, instructing me to kneel before the flames. 'What is your purpose on this Earth?'

I had neither been to church, nor really prayed, but there in the backcountry of Monument Valley, where the Navajo still live the old ways without running water or electricity, I felt compelled, maybe for the first time in my life, to speak instinctively and absolutely from my heart. I spoke of my wife, my children. I asked not to carry my darkness into their lives, to be stronger, to be a better man.

As the words spilled out of my mouth, his chanting grew louder and more intense. Dust devils rattled the walls around us like thunder. Suddenly, I heard my name called and a flood of emotion washed over me. When I looked up, the medicine man was smiling. 'This power is strong,' he said, 'it comes from the Earth.'

By Aaron Millar

The Take Away

The experience opened up a doorway to my own spirituality, one that is inspired, as theirs is, by a reverence for the Earth. The Navajo call it *The Beauty Way*: 'with beauty before me may I walk, with beauty behind me may I walk, with beauty above me may I walk, with beauty all around me may I walk.'

The Build Up

Although it is pretty rare for an outsider to be allowed to take part in a medicine man ceremony such as this one, it's not impossible. The website discovernavajo. com is a good place to start; owned and operated by the tribe, it provides an excellent resource of native-run tourism businesses on the reservation.

It's also possible to explore much of the Navajo Nation independently. Spread out across 70,000 sq km (27,000 sq miles) of Arizona, Utah and New Mexico, its highlights include the petroglyphs and heartbreaking history of Canyon de Chelly, one of their most sacred landscapes; the legends and stunning red rock mesas of Monument Valley, where this ceremony took place; and the spectacular cliff dwellings of Mesa Verde National Park. The latter is just outside the reservation in southern Colorado, built by the predecessors of the Navajo, the Anasazi, almost 1000 years ago – it's one of the best preserved examples of Native American culture in the country.

Left: Monument Valley, land of legend to the Navajo

5

FINDING LIFE ON THE TOUR DU MONT BLANC

THE ALPS, FRANCE, ITALY & SWITZERLAND

'I just need to catch my breath,' I said, as I flopped by the trailside, inhaling a deep lungful of pine-scented air. Ahead, Mont Blanc and the jawbone ridges of the Grand Jorasses and the Aiguille du Midi posed for a family portrait, while behind me dramatic contours, cols and glittering lakes accented just how far I had come. It was an extraordinary panorama, creating a funfair-like, heart-in-mouth excitement, and the blood rushed to my head with dizzying effect. I was above the clouds, but my scuffed hiking boots were still firmly on the ground. These were mountains that punched straight to the viscera. I was a 72-year-old bomb-in-boots, tired and recovering from a life-threatening stroke, and yet I was one last corkscrew descent away from circumnavigating the Mont Blanc massif. The endorphin-rush of completing such a life-affirming journey crackled through my veins like a shockwave. Touring Europe's highest peak had been a lifelong dream, a hut-to-hut exercise in splendour, but also one of companionship with my 36-year-old son. Together, we had hiked 170km (106 miles) and ascended 10,000m (33,000ft) in three countries, achieving something we thought impossible in my twilight years – the giddy feeling would last for days. After one last breath, it was time to come down. I could sense the raw exhilaration that lay over the horizon, but I lingered on the trail. This was a feeling I wanted to savour for a moment longer, to capture a little of the mountain's soul to take home with me.

By Ian MacEacheran

The Take Away

Journey's end should have represented a validation: I was a grandaddy, on one last adventure with the grandaddy of the Alps. But besides the excitement, the peek-a-boo panoramas, and afternoon beer stops on the back of farmers' wagons, it was also a beginning. A chance – and reminder – to live again.

The Build Up

Trekking the Tour du Mont Blanc (autourdumontblanc.com) normally takes between seven and 11 days depending on fitness levels. Most people begin in the resort of Chamonix, at the base of Mont Blanc in France, before following the classic anti-clockwise route over a number of high-altitude passes. The crossing into Italy tackles the heart-pulsating Col de la Seigne (2516m/8255ft), while the more physically demanding ascent into Switzerland, on the homeward leg back to France, confronts the precipitous Fenêtre d'Arpette (2665m/8743ft) – the highest point on the circuit. Plan to hike between five to seven hours a day, but knowing what awaits you along the trail is motivation enough.

Unsurprisingly, with limited accommodation at such altitude, competition for dorm beds at remote refuges is fierce, particularly during the main hiking season, June to September. The trail requires no registration or permit, but it is advisable to book at least one or two nights' in advance: the communal dining and camaraderie at the most in-demand hostelries are another highlight of the trip.

Left: abundant forest clothes the slopes of Mont Blanc in summer
Below: an Alpine overlook affords view of Europe's highest peaks

6

WITNESSING MANDELA'S FIRST FREE SPEECH

CAPE TOWN, SOUTH AFRICA

Aged just 19, I was travelling in Cape Town when an announcement the world had been waiting for was released: Nelson Mandela would finally be freed. Although everyone I'd met advised me against it, I knew I had to witness his first speech.

Walking towards City Hall, the noise was the first thing I encountered – it was emanating from the estimated 250,000-strong crowd in the Grand Parade. I then saw the cordon of armoured riot police trying to stop the flow of people. Somehow I managed to jostle through and join the sea of bodies.

Despite being a pasty-faced Yorkshireman, and the fact I couldn't see any other white faces in the crowd besides a BBC camera crew, I was never scared. In fact, I felt something I'd not experienced before (nor since) – an energy that pulsed and tingled through my entire body. Everything was so raw and in focus: the smell of sweat and alcohol; the vivid black, green and yellow colours of the ANC everywhere; the hypnotic chanting in a language I didn't understand; and the hugs I received from everyone.

When Mandela arrived the explosion of noise actually took my breath away. Although I was bathing in the joy of the situation, I couldn't actually see much through the heaving crowd. That was until I was beckoned by a young South African man to join him perched atop some traffic lights. After a warm embrace, we watched Mandela speak, and the crowd party, until the light began to fade.

By Duff Battye

The Take Away

Looking back, to witness such a pivotal moment in the life of this great man and in the history of South Africa was both humbling and awe inspiring. It also taught me to trust my instincts, and embrace where they take me – on that day it was magic.

The Build Up

Although Mandela is sadly no longer with us, his life is still very much intertwined with the country he sacrificed so much for. For many South Africans, the memory of him and his core values are entrenched in their hearts and minds, and continue to shape their lives. For the visitor, his influence is made obvious by the many places in which he is immortalised.

The most well-known site associated with Mandela in Cape Town is Robben Island, the prison island located in Table Bay – it was here that he spent 18 of his years behind bars. Now a Unesco World Heritage Site, it can be visited on daily tours (robben-island.org.za).

Noble Square in Cape Town's Victoria & Alfred Waterfront also pays tribute to him – here a bronze statue of Nelson Rolihlahla Mandela shares the stage with three other key figures, also Noble Peace Prize laureates, involved in South Africa's journey towards democracy: Nkosi Albert Luthuli, Archbishop Emeritus Desmond Tutu and former State President FW de Klerk.

Grasping the importance of Mandela's first free speech, the City of Cape Town now has plans afoot to place a life-sized statue of him on the very balcony he spoke from on the 11th of February 1990.

Left: the great man on 11 February 1990, free at last after 27 years in captivity
Top: Newspaper headlines proclaim the day

7

BEWITCHED BY LIONS

GIR NATIONAL PARK, GUJARAT, INDIA

Our open jeep bumped along the narrow dirt road through the teak forest of Gir National Park. I'll be honest, I was not overly thrilled to have been woken up at daybreak to visit a park where sightings of the rare Asiatic lion were exceedingly rare. Our guide pointed out some butterflies. My travel partner yawned. The first thing to catch my attention was a bolting wild boar – the black, bristly beast barrelled ahead of us as if its life depended on it. Why?

A sudden flash of something golden next to us made it obvious. A lioness leapt dramatically onto the road and pounced on its prey, with the pair rolling in the dust, one wrestling for control, the other for escape. The look on my guides' faces matched ours – eyes wide, jaws dropped,

speechless – and told me that this was unusual. The squealing clamour soon ended when the cat's jaws clamped down on the boar's bloodied throat.

Hearing a subtle sound on the other side of the jeep, I instinctively turned... there, standing an arm's length away, was a tall and magnificently maned male lion, his bewitching eyes staring straight into mine. This was the Asiatic lion – one of the last of its kind. He looked proud. He looked powerful. It was all I could do not to reach my hand out to him.

Our stare lasted only a moment or two, but it felt like a lifetime. And then he was gone, melting back into the trees before anyone else had even noticed his presence.

By Korina Miller

The Take Away

Sitting between a lion and his mate with his lunch could have been gory and, quite frankly, terrifying. It was, instead, a moment of pure beauty. It made me aware of how far we have removed ourselves from nature in its wildest form and what a privilege it is to witness it.

The Build Up

The 1412 sq km (545 sq mile) Gir National Park (girnationalpark. in) is the last refuge of the Asiatic lion. Located between the cities

of Veraval and Junagadh in Gujarat, the park is accessed from the village of Sasan Gir. Buses run there from Veraval (one hour) and Junagadh (two hours) throughout the day. Second-class, unreserved-seating trains also run to Sasan Gir from Junagadh (2¾ hours) and Veraval (1½ hours).

The best time to visit the park is between December and April, but the park is open from mid-October to mid-June. Three-hour jeep safaris run three times daily (6.30am, 9.30am and 3.30pm),

with the price set at ₹4800 for weekdays, and ₹6000 on weekends.

As there is a restriction on the number of park entry permits available daily, it is worth booking in advance. There are a number of lodges near the village, the top pick being the thatched-roofed Asiatic Lion Lodge (asiaticlionlodge.com).

Right: the population of Asiatic lions in the protected Gir National Park now numbers more than 500; the animals were close to extinction in the mid-20th century

8

TOUCHING HISTORY AT THE WESTERN WALL

JERUSALEM, ISRAEL & THE PALESTINIAN TERRITORIES

Countless hands were caressing Jerusalem's Western Wall, which blushed gold in the late afternoon sun. I watched as women pressed their tear-stained cheeks against the wall, planting kisses on its bare stone.

Standing a few feet back, I struggled to wrap my mind around the Western Wall's history over the past two millennia. It supports the outer part of Temple Mount, where the Second Temple stood before its destruction in 70 AD. Built from hand-chiselled blocks up to 14m (46ft) in length, it's a wonder of ancient architecture. To Jewish people, this is the holiest place of prayer on Earth. It's also part of the world's most contested sacred site: to Muslims, the Buraq Wall, as it's called, adjoins the Noble Sanctuary, the holiest place in Islam after Mecca and Medina.

With a flutter of trepidation, I stepped forwards and placed my palms on the sun-warmed stone. Every fissure in the wall was jammed with tightly folded pieces of paper. Some had fallen onto the ground, unfurling to reveal prayers of joy, despair and gratitude in innumerable languages. Many people believe that prayers placed in the wall's cracks are channelled directly to God. Squeezing my eyes shut, I marvelled at my tiny place within this tide of pulsating humanity. Moments passed – time is impossible to measure at the Western Wall.

Overwhelmed by the crowd, I finally stepped back from the wall. Worshippers flowed around me to fill every available space. I could hear women's murmurs of prayerful longing rising to a crescendo. My heart thudded its reply.

By Anita Isalska

© Anno | Shutterstock, © Mark Millan | 500px

The Take Away

Facing the Western Wall in a crowd of different nationalities and faiths, I experienced a moment of unity that felt precious and powerful. I'm one human being, on this planet for the blink of an eye – but for a fleeting moment in this ancient place I felt a foothold in something eternal.

The Build Up

Regular *sherut* (shared taxi) services depart from Tel Aviv Ben Gurion Airport. Within an hour, you'll be in the heart of busy modern Jerusalem. Enter the Old City through Jaffa Gate and stroll along lively, market-lined David St. Walk downhill and east, guided by signs to the Western Wall.

Passing through a security gate and metal detectors, you'll descend to the Western Wall plaza. The Western Wall is accessible for 24 hours a day, every day of the year. Access is separated by sex (men to the left, women to the right). All visitors must cover from collarbone to knees. Many women wear shawls over their heads, but it isn't obligatory. Men must cover their heads; paper skullcaps are available for visitors who don't have their own.

Shabbat (sunset on Friday to sunset on Saturday) is especially atmospheric, when local Jewish families arrive dressed in their finest attire. During Shabbat, there are restrictions on writing and using electronics in the plaza, following Jewish custom – so sit back and absorb the sacred atmosphere...

Above: the Old City of Jerusalem at sunset
Left: a woman prays at the Western Wall, or the Buraq Wall to Muslims

9

CARNIVAL'S WAVE OF ALEGRÍA

RIO DE JANEIRO, BRAZIL

It was already dark when I awoke. Ash Wednesday loomed, and so did my deadline. I had to write my daily 750-word dispatch about the previous night's excesses. I'd already described a rain-soaked Sambódromo, where Carnival's marquee parade had gobsmacked us for eight straight hours. I'd written about an impromptu rave on Ipanema Beach – usually dangerous after dark, and yet we'd danced in perfect safety next to a boom box until the pink sunrise. I described a tiny bloco (street party with percussion-heavy band and endless beer) that was so rollicking and welcoming that we blew off a fancy ball thrown by Rio's drag royalty.

But now it was Tuesday. I had a colossal hangover and the first symptoms of the melancholy that sweeps Rio when Carnival ends. Then I heard the approach of our neighbourhood's bloco. I rushed down to the street, and soon my blues were transformed into that sweet fruit of Carnival: alegría.

My neighbours – everyone from macho gangsters and transwomen to beachfront millionaires and residents of the hillside slum a few blocks away – flooded the street. A tiny girl sambaed furiously next to her proud mother. At an open window, an old woman bounced in her wheelchair, throwing up her skinny arms in delight.

Suddenly I was weeping. But why? Because I'd seen into the generous heart of Carnival, when alegría is everyone's God-given right. How could I translate that word in English? Happiness is a poor substitute. Jubilation comes closer. It only flourishes when consciously cultivated and extravagantly shared.

By Robert Landon

The Take Away

Until that day, I approached Carnival as the perfect chance to get my own personal jollies – drink like a foolish fish and make out with a dozen strangers. It took a thousand of my neighbours, united in a single wave of *alegría*, to show me Carnival's higher aim.

The Build Up

A floating holiday, Carnival can take place anytime from early February to mid-March. That said, related events begin in December and January, reaching their heights during the four days before Ash Wednesday.

Millions flock to Rio de Janeiro at this time, so plan travel and accommodation as far in advance as possible – and expect to pay a premium. *Blocos* and other events are largely clustered near Ipanema and Copacabana beaches, along the waterfront of the Gloria neighbourhood, and in the central bohemian district of Lapa. Consider making your base in one of these places.

Don't miss the show at the Sambódromo, Carnival's official parade grounds. The ticketing system is too complex to manage from abroad. However, you can get last-minute seats from travel agents, especially in the Copacabana neighbourhood. Shop around; prices vary widely.

A few caveats. First, prepare for extreme traffic. Take Rio's limited but excellent subway whenever possible. Second, remember that Carnival takes place in Brazil's high summer. Stay hydrated (beer, water, repeat). Also, slather on sunscreen and wear light, loose-fitting clothes. Finally, only leave home with that which you are willing to lose to pickpockets; hide emergency funds in your sock, bra or underwear.

Left: thousands of revellers take part in the 'Banda de Ipanema' (traditional carnival band parade) along Ipanema Beach, Rio de Janeiro
Below: the Carnival's Champion's Parade rolls through the city's vast Sambódromo

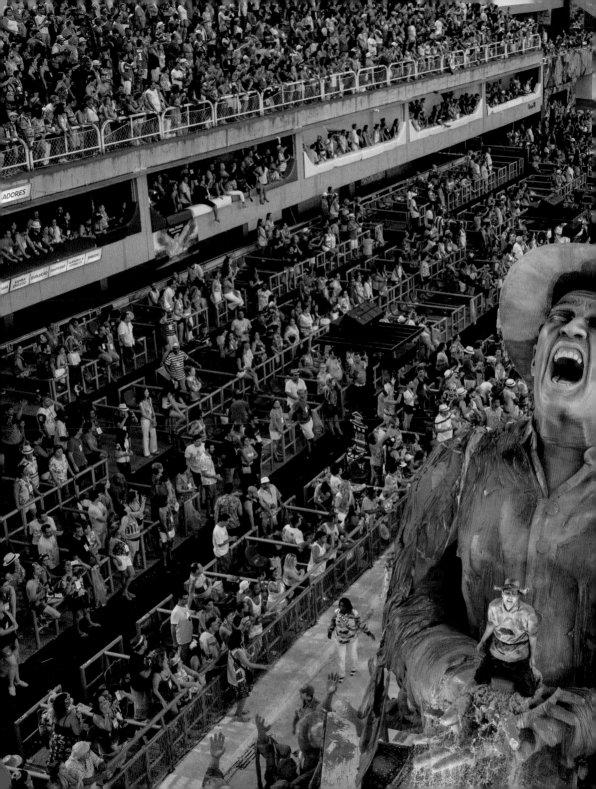

10

STORIES OF THE TRANS-SIBERIAN RAILWAY

BEIJING, CHINA TO MOSCOW, RUSSIA

I was nosing around a paint-peeled train station near Lake Baikal on my Trans-Siberian Railway trip. Keeping the grease-smeared locomotive in sight – I never knew how long these pit stops would last – I watched transfixed as a gaggle of local women tried on fur coats hawked by some travelling merchants. Laughing and strutting, they had no intention of buying but they knew how to have a good time.

Rejoining my girlfriend in our drab, Formica-lined little cabin, I feverishly jotted the scene into my journal. It was the first of many long, rapidly scribbled entries.

After a bleary-eyed year teaching English, we'd dragged ourselves onto the Trans-Siberian in Beijing. We wanted to recuperate and decide what to do next with our lives. On this six-night Moscow-bound trundle, rocking to sleep under gold-streaked sunsets, thinking was a perpetual pastime.

Autumnal larch trees and painted wooden houses flashed past, as we talked of the future, avoided the angry-looking provodnitsa attendants and gorged on baked fish or buttered potatoes from friendly station vendors.

I also filled my dog-eared journal with microscopic handwriting, fearful of exhausting the pages before journey's end. Eventually, as smoky factories and grubby terraced houses slid into view, we crawled into cold, mist-fingered Moscow.

By then, my detangled brain had made a life-changing decision, consigning my teaching career to the buffers. Weeks later, I felt a jolt of excitement when my Trans-Siberian travel story appeared in a London newspaper. A new track had opened ahead of me – and I've been writing ever since.

By John Lee

Trans-Siberian passengers are served by provodnitsa

The Take Away

I realised that every decision I'd ever made,
even the spectacularly bad ones, had
led to that moment of a lifetime.

The Build Up

Most journeys to Antarctica will likely first involve
a stop in Buenos Aires, Argentina, from where it is
a 3½-hour flight to Ushuaia at the southernmost
tip of the Americas. The two-day ocean voyage
across the Drake Passage will begin from there.

This journey is only possible from November to March,
after which Antarctica is reclaimed by impenetrable
ice and darkness. When booking a trip, there are a
few key things to consider: the length of the itinerary,
the size of the ship and the expertise of the guides.

Remember that four days are spent making the two
crossings, so an 11-day trip will mean just a week in and
around the continent. With regards to the vessel's size, a
general rule is that the smaller, the better. This is because
the number of people that are allowed ashore at any
time is limited to 100, which means ships with more than
this number of passengers will need to make them take
turns – thus reducing each person's overall time ashore.

Lastly, even if you don't care about the difference
between a gentoo and an adélie penguin, a team
of marine biologists, historians, and geologists
aboard adds to the experience immensely.

Left: the Milky Way illuminates the
southern sky over Antarctica
Above: as darkness sets in, the half
moon rises over the ocean and ice sheets

PUTTING FEAR TO BED ON THE CAMINO

CARRION DE LOS CONDES, SPAIN

Nothing about my Tuesday morning outside the dusty village of Carrion de los Condes in the north of Spain announced that the day ahead held anything other than the same hot, lonely trudge through the parched wheat fields of the high plains as the day before, and the day before that.

My 500 mile journey along the Camino de Santiago had started in southern France. I crossed the Pyrenees, unpacked my blisters in Pamplona, traded in my heavy leather hiking boots for a pair of red Nike walking shoes in Logroño, and shuffled on – each day more solitary and miserable than the last.

Sure, I had met people from Europe and Australia, South America and Asia – a global community of walkers – yet increasingly I found myself isolating from other travellers. Usually I ate alone, often I found small private lodgings instead of the dorm-like refugios that most pilgrims slept in, and always, always, I walked alone. I became increasingly trapped inside a self-imposed isolation that was far too familiar.

All that time walking alone gave me time to think, too much time. And the thoughts that kept returning in a loop were versions of the same self-lacerating doubt that had plagued me for a lifetime, but now, with only the rhythm of my steps for company, there

was nothing to distract my addled mind. I thought daily of quitting, giving up this fool's errand and returning home, but I kept on.

About halfway along the Camino, the walker comes upon the high meseta, and its mile after mile of wheat. Without warning, I dropped to this parched ground and began weeping. Why I had fallen to my knees sobbing I had no idea. I simply knew that I could not walk another step living the way that I was. Something, anything, had to change.

Through my tears I could see a single black bird circling overhead. When eventually my tears subsided, I retrieved my walking stick – cast aside

Galicia, northwest Spain, is where the journey ends

© Tichr | Shutterstock. © Justin Foulkes | Lonely Planet

Above: pilgrims on Camino de Santiago pass through Sarria in Galicia

The symbol of the Camino is a scallop shell

in my tantrum – and shuffled on.

The next morning I woke and set out again. I felt as if I was forgetting something so I stopped to double-check my pack. I had everything, yet the feeling persisted. An hour into my walk I sat on a plank beside a barn to drink some water. I was conscious of feeling unusually sensitive to my surroundings. There was the faintest of breezes. Then an awareness descended, slowly, as if draping itself down from the sky – and I knew.

What I didn't have, what I had left that morning without, was something that had been with me for as long as I had memories, something that had been so ever present in my life that I was

not aware of its existence until this moment of its first absence. Fear, my nemesis and master, had been revealed – and it had been lifted.

I felt like myself in a way that I never had but knew as deeply familiar. I felt myself awake. And things have never been the same.

By Andrew McCarthy

The Take Away

Halfway along the Camino de Santiago, a realisation by the side of a barn separates my life into 'before' and 'after'.

The Build Up

Rather than a single path, the Camino de Santiago actually comprises several different pilgrimage routes that traverse Spain. What they have in common is that they all converge in holy Santiago de Compostela.

Although some of the lesser-known caminos are becoming increasingly popular, the most famous remains the Camino Francés – it meanders some 790km (490 miles) across northern Spain, and takes most people about a month to complete.

Many people choose to start their pilgrimage on this route in St-Jean Pied de Port, a stunning old walled town in the rolling foothills on the French side of the Pyrenees, just 8km (5 miles) from the border with Spain. The village is just over an hour by train from Bayonne and Biarritz-Anglet-Bayonne airport, which is served by numerous European airlines.

If you don't have a month to spare, but still want to receive a 'Compostela' certificate demonstrating that you completed a camino, you need to walk at least the last 100km (62 miles) of the route – for most this means starting out at the village of Sarria, 114km (70 miles) east of Santiago de Compostela.

A pilgrim's trip home is significantly more straightforward, with Santiago being well connected to the rest of Spain and Europe by air, rail and bus networks.

Right: where the pilgrims are headed – Catedral de Santiago de Compostela
Below left: walkers collect stamps en route to verify the journey
Below right: weary legs in the country lanes of northern Spain

© Justin Foulkes | Lonely Planet

13

PASSING THE FLINCH TEST

SAMBURU NATIONAL RESERVE, KENYA

'There is an etiquette to approaching elephants,' said Saba Douglas-Hamilton, the glamorous chatelaine of Elephant Watch Camp. 'You never encroach on their space,' she continued. 'Instead you let them make the decisions.' As the daughter of Iain Douglas-Hamilton, the world's leading authority on elephant behaviour, she should know, having spent all her life in the company of East Africa's giant pachyderms.

Even so, I hoped she was right because standing right in the path of our open-topped Land Cruiser was a large bull elephant. 'That's Edison,' she said, and it was all too apparent that Edison was in musth. Stoked up with testosterone and desperate to mate, it is the time when elephant bulls can be seriously tetchy.

Saba killed the ignition and Edison strode towards us, extending the tip of his trunk until it was hovering only an inch away from me. Slowly he followed the outline of my body until I could feel his warm breath on the side of my face. Then, inexplicably, he brushed past and stood behind us, his tusks and trunk laid at full length on our canvas roof.

Time seemed to stop. In the silence I could hear wood doves calling all around us. Then he was gone, a giant shadow drifting away through the trees. 'Well done,' whispered Saba. 'You passed the flinch test with flying colours.'

By Brian Jackman

The Take Away
What made this moment so unforgettable for me was the total trust required between all three participants – two humans and one elephant.

The Build Up
Elephant Watch Camp (elephantwatchportfolio.com) is the dream created by Saba's mother, Oria Douglas-Hamilton. It is hard to imagine anywhere with greener credentials than this camp built with dead trees knocked down by elephants. Shaded by giant acacias, it stands on the banks of the Ewaso Nyiro River just a few miles from the headquarters of Save the Elephants, the organisation founded in 1993 by Iain, Oria's husband, who has been studying elephants since the 1960s. In the course of his research he has got to know more than 900 elephants, both residents and sporadic visitors, all of which have been given names and separated into families. Saba can identify them all, and so can her expert guides who, dressed in their traditional tribal finery, will drive you within touching distance of the Samburu herds.

As you might imagine for somewhere offering such a unique experience, Elephant Watch Camp prices are not cheap. Safarilink (safarilink.com) operates two daily flights to Samburu from Nairobi's Wilson Airport. The flight takes less than two hours and representatives of Elephant Watch Camp will meet you at the airstrip.

Left: elephant close-ups are commonplace in Samburu National Reserve

14

LOVE, LIGHT AND TREKKING IN TIBET

SAMYE MONASTERY, TIBET

The wooden door of the monastery pulled back, and a saffron-robed monk popped his head round, a flash of teeth welcoming me inside. This was a mystical, soul-lifting place – I could tell that by the gently spinning prayer wheels and the rainbow flags fluttering in the courtyard. But what I hadn't expected was this spine-tingling sanctuary, with its sand-painted mandalas and hushed meditative chanting, was where I would find inner peace. And fall in love.

I had long been inspired to tackle the 80km (50 mile) trek from Ganden to Samye, a pilgrim route marrying two of the Himalayas' greatest monasteries, and Heinrich Harrer's Seven Years in Tibet had further stirred my spirit while I was volunteering in Lhasa. I had the first view of the region's most ancient Buddhist monastery as my trek came to its potent climax. Seen from a distance, it was a streak of gold on white and crimson, intensified by a divine blue sky – as starkly beautiful as anything I could have dreamt.

Such heightened emotion was eclipsed that night when my eyes caught those of a fellow traveller. In a candlelit room, perfumed by smoky incense, it felt as if the monastery had come to a standstill. Towards midnight, we watched a slew of stars rise over the gompa's majestic terrace together, the lump in my throat a balloon ready to burst. And just when I thought my heart couldn't beat faster, he reached over and kissed me. We were alone and – for a split-second – I could have stayed in that moment forever.

By Katalin Thomann

Monks in Samye, the focus of Katalin's challenging pilgrimage

The Take Away

A tussle of emotions always seems at play when thinking of Tibet. I learnt that the hardest destinations to reach can be the most rewarding, and that romance can hide in the most unexpected of places. Little did I know then, but 10 years later we would marry – and two would become three.

The Build Up

Although Tibet is open to visitors, the Chinese government maintains strict control over who can travel around the autonomous region – and organising a visa and tour can be daunting. Before booking a flight, or a train ticket from Beijing to the capital Lhasa, visitors must first apply for a Tibet Tourism Bureau (TTB) permit from a registered tour company or agency. Free in principle, most companies will charge an administration fee. To complicate matters,

travel outside Lhasa requires an additional Aliens' Travel Permit (ATP), issued by the Public Security Bureau. Bear in mind you need to decide your itinerary beforehand and independent travel is not allowed.

To keep costs manageable, a number of operators arrange small group tours with regular departures in season (from April to October). The most popular trips are to Everest Base Camp and Namtso Lake, as well as the five-day, bucket-list trek between Ganden and Samye.

For travellers who are arriving in Tibet from Nepal, the long-closed border at Kerung-Rasuwa has now reopened, meaning that the classic once-in-a-lifetime route along the fabled Himalayan highway can once again get your pulse racing.

Below: Samye is Tibet's most ancient Buddhist monastery

ENCOUNTERING KUCHI NOMADS

CENTRAL AFGHANISTAN

The roads were so diabolical that our driver – in the hope of reducing the bone-jarring bouncing – actually asked us to get out and collect rocks to put in the back of our vehicle as ballast. We were crossing Afghanistan's mountainous centre to the ancient Silk Road City of Herat, but the trip was a long way from the romance of that storied trade route. The high passes and gravel riverbeds had merged into one continuously bumpy blur. We passed the dinosaur remains of armoured vehicles left destroyed by Afghanistan's modern wars, and observed forts sacked by Genghis Khan. Everywhere the landscape seemed to display its scars.

And then, after passing through a village where a team of oxen were being used to thresh wheat, we saw them. Kuchi nomads. Leading the way, and throwing up a cloud of dust, was a great mass of sheep and goats. Keeping them in check was a group of herding dogs and some children trotting along atop donkeys. Behind them were long strings of camels ridden by women wearing brightly embroidered dresses. Other camels bore black woollen tents and some extraordinary saddlebags made of carpets that you would expect to see in an antique shop, guarded over by weather-beaten men with handsome turbans.

The stresses of the trip melted away. I felt transported to the world of Marco Polo, to a world I assumed no longer existed, and it felt like an enormous privilege to be taken there. Minutes later they were gone, but the experience stays with me to this day.

By Paul Clammer

The Take Away

In Kabul it had been hard to escape the echoes of Afghanistan's recent conflicts. But deep in the mountains I came across an Afghan culture still proud of its traditional life. Looking away from the headlines showed me there was always something new to learn about a country.

The Build Up

Should security concerns permit it (and they currently don't), the drive across central Afghanistan from Bamiyan to Herat takes a minimum of four days, although six or seven days is more realistic.

The highlights include the lapis-blue lakes of Band-e Amir and the dizzying 65m-high Minaret of Jam, which is Afghanistan's only Unesco World Heritage site. The road quality ranges from poor to painfully bad. A 4WD with a trusted local driver is required, but you can still expect to get out and walk up steep stretches, and to collect rocks (for ballast or to put under your vehicle's wheels to help it ford rivers). The route can normally only be tackled between May to October, although early snow or a late spring-melt can still cause problems within these dates. Local transport tends to start winding down for the winter in November, when the high passes will start to close.

Accommodation on the route is restricted to *chaikhanas* (teahouses), where for the price of dinner you're allocated a space on the communal floor to sleep with your blanket. In some remote places available food may be limited to bread, eggs and green tea so bring extra supplies.

Left: Wearing traditional embroidered dresses, a group of Kuchi nomad women in Afghanistan.

16

CLIFF CAMPING IN COLORADO

ROCKY MOUNTAIN NATIONAL PARK, COLORADO, USA

It was a moment most would dismiss as a dream, perhaps even a hallucination. There was an ethereal quality to it, a whiff of the spirit guide. The hummingbird hovered inches from my face like Tinkerbell, its heart throbbing at 1200 beats a minute. And as we gazed curiously at each other, suspended mid-abyss over the rocks and trees hundreds of feet below, I noticed my own adrenaline-ravaged heart finally starting to slow. I took a deep breath. There may be six hours till dawn, but I knew now that I'd make it.

I'd never been remotely afraid of heights before, but that night, lying on a tiny portaledge up a sheer cliff, I was gut-wrenchingly terrified. Cliff camping has become popular for a number of reasons, not least the spectacular ringside seat it affords for sunrise and sunset. But for me it was the darkness. Staring into the black of night during those sleepless hours, watching the moon climb and fall as a forest murmured beneath me, I experienced genuine clarity. It was a night for undisturbed soul searching, for self-reflection, and for a remarkably clear-headed perspective on past, present and future. And while the sunrise was sensational – a roaring inferno of colour tearing across the sky, igniting the Rocky Mountains around me – I was still thinking of the hummingbird, the moon and of the wisdom of the heavens as I abseiled to the ground in the early morning light. That tireless night hanging on the cliff was nothing short of a personal awakening.

By Jonathan Thompson

Jonathan lies on a portaledge where he spent a sleepless night 200m up a cliff

The Take Away

Terrifying and humbling, a night of cliff camping showed me the outer edges of both courage and fear. It made me appreciate so many things in my life that I made a long list of them while teetering up there in the darkness.

The Build Up

Kent Mountain and Adventure Centre (KMAC; kmaconline.com) in Estes Park, Colorado, offers overnight cliff camping from US$800 per person, based on two sharing. That price includes dinner, breakfast, guides and all equipment.

You don't need any previous climbing experience to participate: just a basic level of hiking fitness and a head for heights.

The experience begins at KMAC's headquarters in Estes Park, which is about 90 minutes' drive from Denver. There you'll learn basic rope and abseiling skills, before having lunch with your guides. That afternoon, you'll be driven to nearby Rocky Mountain National Park, where it's a short hike up to Cathedral Rock – your destination for the night. From there, you'll be harnessed up and will begin the steep hike around the back of the cliff face, before abseiling down to your portaledge for the night.

It's a good idea to book a nearby hotel for the following night, so you can head straight there and shower after your descent. The historic Stanley Hotel (stanleyhotel.com), which coincidentally was the setting for Stephen King's *The Shining*, is a short drive away. For more information, see visitestespark.com.

Top: getting ready for a night on the ledge in the Rockies, Colorado

17

PACIFIC PERSPECTIVE

VATULELE, FIJI

From the private two-seater plane, the island of Vatulele looked like a classic South Pacific paradise. Yet, I was apprehensive. Having an exclusive luxury retreat on a remote and sacred island, where 1000 Fijians still live traditional lives, seemed an uncomfortable mix.

At first I wallowed in the resort's free-flowing champagne and seafood gloss. Soon, however, I wanted to explore. I visited the village, comprised of some simple thatched huts amid the palms. Embraced by smiles and welcomes, I quickly found myself in a Fijian church service. Next was a classic male bonding session with a group of village men – squatting on the mud floor of a hut, we shared a wooden cup of kava, a mildly narcotic peppery homemade drink that leaves your face as numb as a dentist's anaesthetic.

Later I wandered to the far shore and sat on a rock next to a fisherman watching the waves. Although it was a truly idyllic scene, I started to feel pangs of guilt relating to the disparity between our levels of affluence.

As if reading my mind, the old weathered chap turned to me and said: 'I feel so sorry for all you visitors. You have to work all year to earn the money to fly halfway around the world to come to a beautiful place like this for a few days. Me, I've got all this every day of my life.'

By Simon Heptinstall

The Take Away

The old fisherman's simple insight changed my attitude to the concept of affluence. Yes, we have microwaves, washer-dryers and satellite TV, but are we really any happier than those without?

The Build Up

Fiji is a group of more than 300 islands in the South Pacific Ocean. It can be reached by direct flights from Australia, New Zealand, Korea, Hong Kong and the USA. Once at Nadi International Airport on the main island of Viti Levu, it's easy to island hop by ferry or light plane.

Reaching and staying on Vatulele Island is dependent on your budget stretching to encompass one of the world's top luxury resorts. However, it's just as easy (and a lot cheaper), to have similar adventures among the famously friendly Fijians on the other islands. There are plenty of beach hotels and resorts for all budgets, but a village homestay (like a B&B) is the best way to get close to the local way of life. And you're never far from the sea wherever you end up.

Left: a wise Fijian fisherman
Top: Fijian beach villas dot the typically paradisal shores of the South Pacific
Above: male villagers mix their intoxicating kava

18

RETRACING THE SLAVE REVOLT

BERBICE, GUYANA

I won't easily forget the Berbice River. Even 80km (50 miles) upstream, it's several hundred metres wide, and winds – jet-black and mirror-calm – through the eerie, whistling jungle. Occasionally, small tin villages would appear, and I'd see people pounding their washing or hacking out canoes. They were all Afro-Guyanese, and my boatmen told me they still had old Dutch names, such as Linden and Amsterdam. Each giant cotton tree, he said, marked the edge of an old slave plantation. But all that had gone, smashed and burnt in the great revolt of 1763.

It was this revolt that had brought me here. I'd spent months studying it in London, picking through old documents. For such a beautiful place it was a bleak tale. In February 1763, the slaves all along the river had risen up, killing their overseers, and helping themselves to whatever they found: muskets, cutlasses, waistcoats and rum. They'd all perish eventually, but for almost a year, they'd looked unstoppable.

Now, 250 years on, I arrived at the ruins of Peereboom. It had been one of Berbice's few brick mansions, and here the planters had made their last stand. Some 2000 barefoot rebels had closed in. In the Dutch accounts, the planters had scattered broken bottles around the house

to deter the attackers. I'd never expected to find much as I climbed the bluff, the air now earthy and sweet. But then – suddenly – all my research burst into life, and there I was, surrounded by thick green chunks of broken glass.

By John Gimlette

© John Gimlette

Setting a course for history up the Berbice River

The neglected grave of a Dutch planter at Peereboom

The Take Away

Amid such haunting magnificence this was an exhilarating moment. For travellers like me, it's an experience you hardly dare hope for, when research, travel and history all come together. I still feel that excitement, that sensation of peeling back the present, and there is the past, as raw as ever.

The Build Up

Independent travel on the Berbice River is possible but difficult. Although there is an inexpensive public ferry that covers some of the distance upriver, transport beyond that, and to the remoter areas, invariably has to be pre-arranged. In Georgetown, Wilderness Explorers (wilderness-explorers.com) can make all the necessary arrangements. Having your own boatman will allow you to stop off at the villages and sites along the way. Not to be missed are the ruins

of Fort Nassau, destroyed in 1763, and still scattered with wreckage and glass.

As for accommodation, there are hotels at the mouth of the river, in New Amsterdam but, after that, you'll find very little. Accommodation in the interior can often only be booked by radio and, again, tour operators such as Wilderness Explorers can make all your arrangements.

The Berbice region is hot, but not unpleasantly so, with the mean temperature in the shade throughout the year being 27°C. The main wet season is from May to June, with another from late December to late January.

Above: on the banks of the Berbice at Peereboom. It was from this landing that the surviving planters and slavers fled the 1763 revolt, under heavy fire

19

FIRST WATCH
ON THE CORAL SEA

LOUISIADE ARCHIPELAGO, PAPUA NEW GUINEA

I was 12 years old and my mum had just given me my first digital watch. Fittingly, I was using it to keep time on my other first watch, a solo pre-dawn stint on the deck of our sailboat as we crossed the Coral Sea from Cairns to New Guinea. I was skippering while my family slept below, and I felt so grown up.

When I went up to the bow to check the ropes, I looked out at the quiet ocean and contemplated the fact that we were two days' sail from anywhere. Raising my gaze above the dim horizon to the heavens above that were lit by stars, I was hyper-aware that it was just tiny me floating on our massive planet.

Later, when I was looking down into the deep water, I saw streamers of tiny lights curling through the darkness. At first I thought it was the reflection of the stars, but I soon realised it was ribbons of bioluminescence stirred up by a pod of dolphins who'd decided to join me. Although they ended up accompanying us alongside our boat for the next day or so, playing at the bow and throwing us coy glances from the water, it was that early morning which I will truly never forget; the ocean, the quiet night and the stars, the animals, me, growing up in the world. Magic.

By Ruth Cosgrove

The Take Away

Travel can make and maintain a sense of wonder that drives everything in a better direction.

The Build Up

The crossing of the Coral Sea from Cairns in Australia's far North Queensland to the Louisiade Archipelago, which extends from the tip of New Guinea, typically takes about five days' sailing, depending on the weather conditions. This trip was undertaken in May, and was the beginning of a six-month-long island-hopping and diving adventure that explored the tropical islands of Papua New Guinea and the Solomon Islands.

Crewing jobs (eg deckhands, cooks, stewards, engineers) on the many private yachts that sail the area (Coastal Queensland, New Guinea and throughout Indonesia) can be found by contacting local yacht clubs, and on sites such as crewseekers.net, vikingrecruitment. com and even gumtree.com. Getting a scuba-diving ticket is recommended as the diving on the reefs that surround the islands of Papua New Guinea is some of the best in the world.

Left: with no land on the horizon, the sky above becomes the moving landscape

20

ON HORSEBACK WITH GAUCHOS

PATAGONIA, CHILE

Patagonian gauchos ride Chile's Torres del Paine

Normally I wouldn't class anyone wearing a beret, scarf and leather chaps as hip, but the Patagonian gauchos I was riding with were definitely the coolest guys on the planet. Trading both cigarettes and knowing wisecracks, their legendary equine skills equipped them perfectly for a working life amid the mountains and steppe of Chile's Torres del Paine National Park. As my mount carefully followed their languid route downhill, a delicate snowfall began to drift through diffuse southern light.

On the edge of epic sub-alpine landscapes, my peripheral vision picked out quicksilver waterfalls and a lake almost concealed in a compact valley. Lured by the lip-smacking promise of a Chilean barbecue, the gauchos' confident and whip-smart posse of dogs bounded ahead to lead the way. Soon the stables came into view and, as the dogs' excitement level peaked, I dismounted to enter a simple pavilion infused with the flavours and aromas of South America.

Chinook salmon from nearby rivers were being carefully steamed, and as two whole sides of lambs were grilled upright in the traditional asado style, a gaucho offered me a rustic tumbler of robust Malbec. I washed down an empanada crammed with meat, olives and egg as he pulled a big knife from his waistband and started carving the perfectly grilled meat. Outside, the snow was now falling heavily, and together with the sheepdog lying at my feet licking his lips, I knew there was nowhere else I'd rather be.

By Brett Atkinson

Tasty empanadas
help to sustain those
on horseback

The Take Away

I'm a big fan of urban travel and vibrant city experiences including street food, restaurants and markets, but riding with the Patagonian gauchos and their loyal dogs reinforced the simple pleasures of slowing down to the pace of natural rhythms amid truly spectacular landscapes.

The Build Up

Explora's Hotel Salto Chico (explora.com) on the shores of Lake Pehoé in the Chilean Patagonia offers horse-riding excursions with the region's gauchos. These adventures begin from the 2 de Enero ranch, a sprawling property of about 60 sq km (23 sq miles). All raised on a family estate in central Chile, the ranch's 26 horses are harnessed for 16 different horse-riding expeditions that range from a half- to a full-day, and are designed for riders of all experience levels. Suitable for beginner riders are the Pampas del Toro and Laguna Linda rides taking in local birdlife or stunning views of the Paine Massif, while the full-day Donoso and Tempanos rides include more challenging aspects such as negotiating wetlands or galloping along plains and rocky terrain.

From September to April as weather permits, the ranch's Quincho (barbecue) facility is used as the end point of some rides, and an outdoor lunch is included on others. To reach Hotel Salto Chico, fly south from the Chilean capital of Santiago to Punta Arenas (about 3½ hours), from where it's a 4½ hour drive.

Below: the mountainous expanse of Torres del Paine National Park, Chile

21

CLIMBING HALF DOME

YOSEMITE NATIONAL PARK, CALIFORNIA, USA

A full moon silvered the silent, snow-patched Sierras as I flopped, exhausted, at the top of Half Dome's sheer northwest face. It was 2am, some 42 hours since we had started climbing, and frost sparkled on the granite crystals of the summit's rocks. My fingers were numb with cold, and I was hungry, thirsty and aching in every muscle. And I had never felt so good.

I had discovered rock climbing as a teenager, and it had swiftly become an obsession – the thrill of exploration, the joy of controlled movement, the challenge of overcoming fear. California's Yosemite Valley was one of the cradles of the sport, and Half Dome was its icon. Its vast, vertical rock face, 671m (2200ft) high, calls to any aspiring rock climber – for me it was a magnet.

As I began taking in the rope to bring up my partner, I thought back on the anticipation and effort that had led me here – six months of training and preparation, a week of warm-up climbs and a four-hour hike to the start of the climb. Two dozen pitches of finger-mangling cracks, airy bridging and technical ropework. A night spent on a ledge barely wider than my waist, a thousand feet off the ground. Stomach-churning exposure, breathtaking views, alternating waves of exhilaration and terror, and

the final three pitches completed by torchlight. And finally, this moment of quiet exaltation, with the starlit peaks of the Sierra Nevada stretching away to the horizon, pregnant with the promise of further adventures.

By Neil Wilson

The Take Away

Succeeding on Half Dome made me feel like anything was possible. The experience inspired me to write my first published magazine article, which ultimately led to me giving up a safe career in the oil industry for the more adventurous life of a travel writer.

The Build Up

The Regular Northwest Face is a serious and committing rock climb, usually completed over two or three days, and suitable for experienced climbers only.

If, as most climbers do, you plan to spend a night at the foot of the climb, you will need a (free) national park wilderness permit.

It is possible for non-climbers to hike to the summit of Half Dome via a route known as The Cables. This path up steep slabs is aided by steps and handrails, and is one of the most popular backcountry hikes in Yosemite (the number of walkers is limited to 300 a day). You will need to obtain a Half Dome Permit (nps.gov/yose/planyourvisit/hdpermits.htm) – most are let through a pre-season lottery held in March, but around 50 per day are made available in a short-notice lottery (US$20; apply two days in advance).

There are several campsites in Yosemite, but Camp 4 is the spiritual home of valley climbing (in 2003 it was added to the National Registry of Historic Places).

Above: the daunting slab of Half Dome's peak rises to an elevation of 2694m (8839ft)
Left: hikers can also take on Half Dome at Yosemite National Park via the Cables route

22

AN ENLIGHTENING ENCOUNTER WITH MOUNTAIN GORILLAS

VOLCANOES NATIONAL PARK, RWANDA

Just when I thought my heart couldn't beat any faster, I cautiously left the forest's grasp and descended into the clearing where a dozen mountain gorillas had been spotted. The intense feelings of anticipation were rapidly replaced by excitement when my eyes caught sight of the first gorilla, a young male basking in the warmth of a brilliant shaft of light. This sighting was followed in short order by another, a hulking 200kg (480lb) silverback standing just 7m (23ft) away. I was absolutely overwhelmed by his size, his stature and his thoughtful gaze. He continued to look on as a youngster, not yet a year old, stumbled out of the undergrowth and approached me. Not far behind were a couple of inquisitive females.

Over the remainder of our hour (the maximum time allowed), I watched the tiny youngster frolic about, beat his chest and sing in delight, all from the distance of several metres. The females took turns grooming, dining on wild celery and studying the happiest human on the planet. During this time the minutest details of their faces, human-like hands and enchanting eyes were permanently engraved into my psyche. My ecstatic smile and uncontainable, childlike giggles halted abruptly when I heard my guide say three small words: 'Time is up.' Just as I was about to plead for a few seconds more, a bolt of lightning struck nearby and the shockwave sent the gorillas scattering into the jungle's depths. A fittingly dramatic end to an encounter that I'll never forget.

By Jane Powell

© David Yarrow | Getty, © Eric Lafforgue | Lonely Planet

The Take Away

Besides indelible recollections of the excitement and energy pulsing through my body during the encounter, what I carry with me today from my hour with the gorillas is the sheer captivation I felt. I wasn't just looking into the eyes of an animal, but rather those of a relative.

The Build Up

Gorilla permits (US$1500) for Rwanda's Volcanoes National Park are available from the Rwanda Development Board (rwandatourism.com) in Kigali, the country's capital. With 10 groups of habituated gorillas, and a maximum number of daily visitors to each being eight, this limits the park's permits to just 80 per day. Unsurprisingly, competition is fierce, particularly during the peak seasons of December to January and July to August. It's also possible to secure a permit months ahead online, or through a registered tour operator.

On the day itself, your journey will began at 7am when you present yourself at the park's headquarters just outside of Musanze. It's at this point that you'll be allocated the particular family group of gorillas. From there you'll be driven to the start of your trek. While some forays into the jungle can be a short stroll, some involve three-hour hikes up steep, muddy slopes through dense vegetation to an altitude over 3000m. Knowing what awaits you is motivation enough, though the combination of excitement, altitude and gradient will certainly have your pulse racing.

Similarly captivating experiences are also possible in Uganda (Bwindi Impenetrable National Park and Mgahinga Gorilla National Park) and the Democratic Republic of Congo (Virunga National Park).

Left: it's the finer details of your encounter that will stick with you the longest
Above: Mt Muhabura is the second-highest peak in Rwanda's Volcanoes National Park

23

ROUSING RESPECT

KŌYA-SAN, JAPAN

The feeling of mystical otherworldliness I had been led to expect from Kōya-san actually began before I had even truly arrived. Stepping off the train at Gokurakubashi Station, I boarded a cable car, which transported me upwards through white mist and green trees. When I arrived at the town itself, the picture was completed by the traditional Japanese architecture of the ubiquitous ryokan, the forest-covered mountains that surrounded me on every side and the saffron-robed Buddhist monks who were walking on the streets. I was struck by how quiet and peaceful it was. Having arrived directly from the bustle and bright lights of Osaka, Kōya-san was a change of pace akin to stepping off a bullet train.

However, I do not choose to remember Kōya-san through the sights I saw or the food I ate. Instead, my experience there was defined by a profound sense of respect. I experienced this when I checked into my accommodation and a softly spoken Buddhist monk with broken English thanked me every time I answered one of his many questions. I witnessed it when I awoke at 5am to participate in a lovingly practised Buddhist prayer service. I felt it when I explored the town and visited its numerous temples, and when I admired the beauty and grandeur of nature and of human endeavour. I was surrounded by it when I wandered through Oku-no-in and its hundreds of sobering memorials. And it deeply challenged the busy self-centredness I perceived as normal by demonstrating an alternative perspective.

By William Allen

The Take Away

Living in a city full of people trying to get ahead in the rat race, it can be easy to think that this simply is what the world is. Kōya-san showed me a different world, one of quiet respect, and challenged me to bring that back to my everyday life.

The Build Up

Without a rental car, access to Kōya-san is via the Nankai Railway from Osaka. Trains from Namba Station (kyūkō; ¥1260, one hour and 40 minutes; tokkyū; ¥2040, 43 minutes) terminate at Gokurakubashi, at the base of the mountain, where you can board a cable car (five minutes, price included in train tickets) up to Kōya-san itself. From the cable car station, take a bus into central Kōya-san; walking is prohibited on the connecting road.

Nankai's Kōya-san World Heritage Ticket (¥3400, covers return train fare, including one-way tokkyū fare from Osaka), buses on Kōya-san and discounted admission to some sites.

If you have a Japan Rail Pass, take the JR line from Kyoto to Hashimoto, changing at Nara, Sakurai and Takada en route. At Hashimoto, connect to the Nankai line to Kōya-san (¥830, 50 minutes). Without a Japan Rail Pass, it's easier and quicker to connect to the Nankai line at Namba.

To continue on from Kōya-san to Hongū on the Kumano Kodō, return to Hashimoto on the Nankai line and transfer to the JR line to Gōjō (¥210, 15 minutes), then continue by bus to Hongū (¥3200, four hours).

Left: a Buddhist statue watches over Okunoin cemetery in Koya-san
Below: Konpon Daito Pagoda at Danjo Garan Temple

24

TEMPLES AT DAWN

BAGAN, MYANMAR

The sky was still an inky black as I struggled to turn on my head torch and find my bike. As I headed out along a sandy track, the stars above started to disappear as the heavens began to lighten. Lone palm trees stood like sentinels for the silhouettes that slyly emerged in the distance. Coated in mist, this sea of temples rose up from the landscape as I approached, and the myriad spires and ornate carvings, stone lions and giant Buddhas soon dominated the skyline.

More and more temples of all shapes and sizes appeared, each bathing in dawn's shimmering shades of gold. Some featured sandstone statues, others imposing stupas and sculptured terraces. A few appeared like monsters from the deep, covered in creepers and overgrowth – it was these beasts among the tamarind trees that I found the most alluring.

As I proceeded on foot, my legs frequently snagging on intruding greenery in the rush to not miss sunrise, I found a barely detectable temple with accessible stone steps. Up I climbed precariously to a narrow terrace below a simple spire, from where I could see the tip of the sun, a burning crimson, just starting to rise. My heart was hammering as I found myself transported into a forgotten world. A magical, mysterious land lost in time, bathed in a palette of fire. All was quiet as the sun rose like a goddess and I was swept back to the centuries when the great kings of Burma ruled.

By Nicky Holford

The Take Away

In that moment, hypnotised by the glowing light flowing through magnificent monuments, a wave of joy swept through me. I felt bewitched. My earlier adrenaline and excitement dissolved. I remember the total silence and amazement. It was a sight I'll never forget.

The Build Up

In its glory between the 9th and 13th centuries, the Kingdom of Pagan (as it was then called) contained more than 10,000 temples, shrines, pagodas and stupas in an area of some 67 sq km (26 sq miles) on the high plains bordered by the Ayerarwady River. Today, 2230 temples have survived. Each has a unique flavour and story to tell, such as the red brick, 12th-century gold-topped Dhammayangyi Buddhist temple – it was built by King Narathu, a ruler who murdered his family and cut off the arms of any worker who failed instructions. Large, elaborately carved Buddhas, tiled panels, murals depicting stories, and a network of complex passages contribute to make the Bagan temples one of the most important archaeological sites in Asia.

Popular sites get overcrowded, so stray further afield to find your sunrise or sunset temple. All visitors to Bagan, 190km (118 miles) south of Mandalay and 690km (430 miles) north of Rangoon, are required to pay an Archaeological Zone fee (K25,000), which is valid for five days and covers the four main settlements of Nyaung U, Old Bagan, Myinkaba and New Bagan. Bikes in varying states of repair are widely available to rent for K2000-8000 per day. An e-bike will set you back K13,500 a day. Hot-air balloon flights cost from US$325 per person for 45 minutes.

Left: navigating the many temples, shrines, pagodas and stupas of Bagan by bicycle is a brilliant option

25

CORAL ISLAND CASTAWAY

HERON ISLAND, GREAT BARRIER REEF, AUSTRALIA

Sitting under the whispering casuarina trees in the dunes above Shark Bay, I lingered after dusk. The noddies were there, as always, flying in close pairs as they skipped across the reef flat. Then other birds appeared among them, soaring and pirouetting through the smouldering embers of sunset. I felt my pulse quicken as first a dozen, then a hundred, then thousands of them gathered in the skies above Heron Island. The wedge-tailed shearwaters had returned! After months of ocean wandering, they had converged en masse to breed on this 29-hectare speck of land.

As darkness fell, I began to hear them crashing through the pisonia trees, landing with a thud on the forest floor. That's when the magic began: the nocturnal song of the shearwater – a crooning, wailing chorus – ebbing and flowing across the island. I walked slowly into the forest and crouched a few feet from a pair already consumed by courtship. They sat facing each other, preening, rattling bills and uttering that haunting song. Nearby, another pair were busy excavating their burrow. The birds seemed oblivious to me. I spent the entire night watching them until, a couple of hours before dawn, they began to make their way towards the dunes. The whoops and yelps of their chorus reached a crescendo, and then I heard the sound of rapidly slapping webbed feet on well-worn sand as shearwaters launched themselves off the dune crests. By sunrise, most had vanished.

By William Gray

The Take Away

On the night the shearwaters arrived, I had been living on Heron for over a month – a voluntary castaway, studying the island's wildlife. It evokes a time when my clock reset to simple cues such as day, night, tide and rhythms of wildlife. It taught me to slow down, pause and look a little while longer.

The Build Up

Scientists at Heron Island Research Station (uq.edu.au) occasionally need volunteers, but a less academic route to the coral cay is to base yourself at Heron Island Resort (heronisland.com). Accommodation (from A$330 per room per night) ranges from double rooms to luxurious suites. Located 89km (55 miles) off the Queensland coast, the island can be reached from Gladstone by boat (A$128 return) or seaplane (A$698 return). Around 35,000 wedge-tailed shearwaters arrive in early October, joining resident black noddies,

reef egrets, buff-banded rails, Capricorn silvereyes and silver gulls. By December, some 100,000 birds are nesting on the island. Shearwater chicks hatch in February; the adults start leaving the island in April, followed by their young in May.

The resort offers ranger-led birdwatching tours, or you can explore on your own, taking care to keep to paths and avoid trampling shearwater burrows. You can view nesting turtles from November to March (the hatchlings emerge from January to early June). Heron Island's spectacular coral reef can be explored year-round (diving, snorkelling, guided reef walks, sea kayaking and semi-submarine tours are all available). Humpback whales are often sighted during July and August.

Above: wedge-tailed shearwaters make their home on Heron Island between October and May
Left: Heron Island, a coral cay, is 89km (55 miles) northeast of Queensland

26

CENTRAL PARK STROLL IN THE SNOW

NEW YORK CITY, USA

I was a naive first-time traveller on a big trip to New York City from my home in Australia. It was the mid-1990s, and despite the 1987 film Wall Street *painting the city as a playground for capitalism's winners, New York was still very much a mecca for aspiring actors, writers and musicians living in studio apartments and freezing warehouse conversions. It was a little bit gritty, everyone talked very loudly and the subway didn't feel very safe to this 21-year-old kid from Melbourne (blame the 1990 thriller* Jacob's Ladder*).*

Before I left home, oodles of older people (my parents' friends and my friends' parents) all told me the same thing: 'Whatever you do, don't walk through Central Park at night.' But one evening after dark I found myself on the wrong side of the park, and being young, stupid and rather reckless, I decided to cut through it anyway.

When I got to the middle I stopped for a moment to look around me. I did a slow 360-degree turn and took it all in: the park was completely white with fresh snow, the only other tracks were a squirrel's dancing around a tree and the apartment windows above were lit up like fairy lights. And then, in the stillness, the snow started to silently fall from the sky and wet my cheeks.

It was a moment of pure beauty and elation. I was in New York. It was magical. And the world seemed full of possibility.

By Tasmin Waby

The Take Away

Sometimes it pays to ignore the wisdom of your elders. Flouting such advice resulted in this magical moment and, as luck has probably been on my side most of my life, it has since led to others. And lastly, beauty can be found wherever you look for it.

The Build Up

Everyone has a different dream of New York City before they arrive, and it rarely fails to deliver – in spades.

Iconic Central Park takes prime position in Manhattan and is impossible to miss. Summer finds the park buzzing with city workers, fitness fanatics and mesmerised tourists. Winter is quieter, but it gets dark early and the trees are without their luxurious canopies.

The city has also added more green spaces in the past decade, with the High Line and the Hudson River Park providing extra great spots for strolling, people watching, and unwinding away from yellow cabs and fast-paced pedestrians.

Accommodation in New York is as diverse as the city itself. Even if you won't spend much time in your room, it's still worth putting in the research to find the perfect place to stay for your budget. If you're staying for more than a few days consider changing accommodation midway so you can live in a different borough for a different NYC experience.

If you're arriving by train or bus, disembark Midtown at Penn Station (Amtrak) or the Port Authority Bus Station (Greyhound) and you'll find yourself immediately in the throng of New York's manic energy.

Left: Snow covers the ground around Gapstow Bridge in New York's Central Park

27

REMOTE MOUNTAIN RESCUE

KYRGYZSTAN

In the Kichi-Kegeti Valley, the mountains retain a permanent cap of snow throughout the year

From our vantage on the valley's slopes, we could see points of light approaching around the mountain's curve until a face finally emerged from the darkness.

Much earlier, after a day and a half under stormy skies, even the steep scree slope below the pass wasn't enough to prompt a second-guessing on a third attempted ascent – it must be the right valley, and dark clouds were moving in fast.

It was meant to be an easy getaway to a lake we'd both been to before, but we were tempted by the unexplored pass beyond to make a rewarding loop. After reaching the crest, a harrowing descent of snow, rocks and a butt-first slide led to a distinct thought: 'I'm glad we don't have to do that again.'

Several hours downhill, atop the sheer face of a waterfall, a nagging suspicion became a growing realisation. This was not the path. Not the way. How do we get out, get home? There was frustration, self-recrimination, but also a quietly gnawing fear of a steep, unsafe, unroped ascent on a pass that we never should have come down.

Miracle mobile phone reception allowed a measured message home that belied our growing concern:
'We won't be home tonight. What's Kyrgyzstan's emergency number?'

A few static-crackled phone calls later, we sat, waited, and hoped help was coming... But darkness fell, and with it our spirits.

That is until that face eventually materialised. After a long drag on his cigarette, a hand was extended along with two simple words: 'I rescuer.' We clipped into harnesses. The feeling, the moment, the relief: all sublime.

By Stephen Lioy

© Stephen Lioy

The Take Away

I think back to this hike any time I prepare for another. Aside from a more-than-mild embarrassment, it's a reminder that the potential for danger is always present, and a backup plan is always essential. Above all: always respect the mountains.

The Build Up

Hikers anywhere in the world should observe basic safety norms: always tell someone where you're going and when you'll return; follow 'leave no trace' principles; and pack the '10 Essentials', namely insulation, illumination, accurate maps, food, water, fire, first aid, sun protection, emergency shelter and a multi-tool.

In mountainous environments, it's essential to also prepare for quickly changing weather patterns and watch for signs of altitude-induced sickness, which manifest in headaches, dizziness, difficulty breathing or nausea. High-altitude edema, whether cerebral or pulmonary, is life-threatening in serious cases.

In Kyrgyzstan, remote mountain environments and limited infrastructure make these tenets even more important. Groups such as Community-Based Tourism (cbtkyrgyzstan.kg), the Trekking Union of Kyrgyzstan (tuk.kg) and Visit Alay (visitalay.kg) organise group hikes for less experienced visitors, but even those accustomed to the terrain should keep information on hand for international embassies and the Ministry of Emergency Situations (☎ 161) in the event of unexpected contingencies. Stretched resources and limited language skills temper the ability of many local rescue groups to respond with alacrity, so independent trekkers should be prepared for self-sufficiency in most mountainous regions of the country.

Left: delayed by weather on day two, Stephen ascends a glacial moraine to the top of Kichi-Kegeti Valley

28

IN THE ARABIAN SANDS

EMPTY QUARTER, OMAN

More than mountains, forests, beaches and oceans, I have always loved deserts. Desert travel somehow brings into sharp focus the essential ingredients of existence: drinking, walking, sleeping. There is a strange spirituality in the silence of the desert. It's no coincidence that Jesus, Moses and Mohammed went into the desert to talk with the Almighty. Or that Luke Skywalker found Obi-Wan Kenobi in the lifeless canyons of Tatooine.

I had been to a great many deserts before, though none quite compared to my visit to the Rub Al Khali – the Empty Quarter. It is the biggest sand desert in the world, an expanse of rolling dunes roughly the size of France, where there are no cities, no roads, no people. I'd become fascinated ever since locating the Empty Quarter on my dad's giant Atlas as a child: an inkless expanse at the heart of the Arabian Peninsula that looks a bit like an error at the printing press, or another kind of ocean.

I joined a guide in the Omani town of Salalah, and set out on the six-hour drive into the interior. Before long, we were among the dunes – great ranges of sand that looked like a turbulent sea frozen in time. In the midday heat, the desert is a fearsome place as shade is non-existent. Around sunset we made camp and I took a walk, and the Empty Quarter was reincarnated as another, kinder landscape – the contours of the dunes cast long shadows, the colours softened to honey-yellow, and I could feel the sand cooling beneath my toes.

By Oliver Smith

Above: camels are a source of both transport and food for desert venturers
Below: Oman's Empty Quarter extends as far as the eye can see

The Take Away
Being in a lifeless place somehow heightens every aspect of being alive. And in such a crowded world, the freedom of roaming in a vast empty landscape could not have been more precious to me.

The Build Up
The Empty Quarter is emphatically not a destination for a desert novice,

and it claims lives each year. There is a significant risk of getting lost, as well as getting stuck in soft sand or quicksand, or getting caught in sandstorms. It is essential to travel in the company of an experienced guide – they should have a tow rope, shovels, sand ladders and other recovery equipment. A GPS and satellite phone is also helpful. Allow for five litres of water per person per day's travelling.

The Empty Quarter is spread across Saudi Arabia, Yemen, Oman and the UAE – but is best geared up for tourism in the UAE and Oman. In Oman, a small number of companies offer multi-night trips from the port town of Salalah – among them Arabian Sands Tours (arabiansandtoursservices.com). Accommodation means staying in traditional Arabian tents, and dining nightly on camel meat and dates. For a more easily accessible desert travel experience, consider Wahiba Sands, also in Oman, or Erg Chebbi in Morocco.

29

BICYCLING BEYOND FEAR

MOROCCO TO GIBRALTAR

The Rock of Gibraltar marks the adventure's end

Below: parts of the 11,000km route were more stunning than others – here, the coastline of Greece

I had to stop pedalling. Not because of the blistering temperatures. Not to differentiate between the sting of tears and the smart of sweat on my sun-raw skin. Not even to recover enough for a full gulp of air. I stopped because beauty overcame me. As I crested a steep hill on that day's bicycle ride, I was stilled by a seeming mirage of multiple depths or a woodblock print made real – layer upon lighter pastel layer of hills stretching into the heat-faded distance.

I stopped too because of a powerful release of emotion. After nearly nine months of resolve-battering riding, my defences had finally disintegrated. And I shed proud and terrified tears of realisation that my 11,000km (6800 mile) bicycle journey from Morocco to Gibraltar, the long way around the Mediterranean Sea, was nearly over. Despite numerous warnings, my teammates and I would accomplish our goal.

The cautions still resonated. Before setting out, we had been repeatedly reminded how we would never survive. Worse, in each country we visited during the trip, we were asked our next destination only to be advised to avoid it because people across the border would commit terrible crimes against us. Which, sure enough, was never actually the case.

In principle, we knew that fear of the unknown distorts perceptions. But it wasn't until that sultry hilltop that I realised how, in practice, we had really and truly conquered fears – our own and others.

By Ethan Gelber

Cycling across the Spanish border for the final push

The Take Away

Sometimes, no matter how much you love or trust people, you should doggedly pursue your chosen path, especially when others' concerns for your wellbeing runs counter to your desires. I listened but, for once, I did not heed, because I knew the concerns were anchored in ill-informed fear, not fact.

The Build Up

An epic bicycle journey – of long distance and duration – takes planning, especially an expedition with a mission. There are physical challenges, material obstacles and lots of emotional turmoil to overcome. The physical challenges are the easiest to face through proper training. Ideally, no one should commence a major bicycle trip without first understanding how the body reacts to extended time in a bike saddle.

The material obstacles depend on the available resources and the scope of a mission. If someone can bankroll his or her own journey, then all is well. However, if a journey's ambition, as declared through a clear mission or purpose, is greater than its assets, then mechanisms for sponsorship and partnership, as well as income-generating plans, may need to be implemented. The latter was the case with the Mediterranean journey, a programme that took nearly three years to pull together and involved scores of local collaborators.

The emotional turmoil is the hardest to manage, especially if one's dearest counsel – family and friends – remains unsupportive. It takes discipline and defences. Just be ready for them to crumble unexpectedly when, near completion of the mission, you encounter a blistering day with unexpectedly gorgeous views.

SWIMMING WITH WHALES

TAHITI ITI, TAHITI

It was a perfect sunny day, with optimal conditions, and there were only three of us scheduled to join our captain and guide in the inflatable boat. After the brief at the dive shop, we embarked and headed towards the eastern tip of Tahiti Iti, the most pristine part of the island. The setting was dramatic to say the least – a cobalt blue ocean with towering basaltic sea cliffs as a backdrop – and the atmosphere truly wild.

That day there was only one boat out there: ours. Then, after about half an hour of fruitlessly searching for the smallest sign of a whale, it happened.

'Two! On the left!' Our guide shouted. 'A mother and a calf!'

I swiftly dropped into the sea and it wasn't long before I saw what looked like an apparition appear. Just a few metres away was a massive humpback, along with its infant calf. I was absolutely mesmerised by the power and grace of these leviathans as they played with each other in the shallows.

At one point the mother gently came closer to me and we shared a glance, me peering into its enormous eyeball. I had no fear. Instead, I had the feeling it was greeting me as if an old friend – it was a deeply moving moment. After about 20 minutes, the pair slowly swam away. I got back on board, totally exhilarated. And as a perfect coda, the mother leapt into the air with its two pectorals open and landed back in the water with a tremendous splash, about 100m off the boat. As if it was waving goodbye.

By Jean-Bernard Carillet

The Take Away

On top of the indelible recollections of the thrill I felt during the encounter, I can say that this experience has turned me into a true lover of whales. Now I feel the urge to go whale watching at regular intervals and I have started planning some trips accordingly.

The Build Up

Most dive shops on the islands of Tahiti, Moorea and Bora Bora lead whale-watching tours between July and October, when humpbacks swim near shore to breed before heading back to the icy waters of the Antarctic.

It's important to book ahead as most outings fill up fast. Prices start at US$70 for a half-day outing, and gear (wetsuit, fins, mask and snorkel) is included. All whale-watching trips should be led by a qualified instructor who will give a comprehensive brief on board prior to immersion. This activity has exploded in recent years, and unfortunately the way some operators conduct trips leaves something to be desired – it's important to stick to established outfits that are ecologically sensitive and follow animal welfare protocols. Check with Mata Tohora (facebook.com/matatohora), which encourages good practice and can give you recommendations.

Some words of warning: whale sightings are not guaranteed; and the sea can be rough, so be prepared.

Left: *a pair of humpback whales. The species can reach a length of around 16m (50ft)*

31

PRE-PARENTHOOD PYRAMID

YUCATAN PENINSULA, MEXICO

I wasn't really supposed to be up here. And, of course, that only added to the thrill. Nohoch Mul is the tallest of the Yucatan Peninsula's Mayan pyramids, and from its 42m (138ft) summit I had a falcon's-eye view of horizon-to-horizon jungle. The cork trees, chit palms and acacias below fused into one rippling, green ocean that submerged the ancient city of Cobá below. It was glorious, but I wasn't really here for the view.

In truth, I hadn't set out to do it. But I couldn't resist the opportunity to prove a point, namely that a seven months' pregnant woman is still a capable human being. (Pity my vertigo-cursed husband, who now felt obliged to accompany wife and soon-to-be-firstborn child.) And now, surveying the world at my feet, I felt invincible.

The same couldn't be said when we had started the upward clamber. Due to the limestone blocks no longer being in mint 7th-century condition, progress was slow as we left the jungle's squawks and shade beneath us. A rope hanging down the structure was the sole concession to safety, and as the pyramid narrowed we discovered that looking sideways was as bad an idea as looking down. But then we were at the summit, exhilarated by the stonking panorama and giddying sense of achievement, and feeling not a little trepidation at what lay ahead. Parenthood, yes, but first, that descent...

By Liz Edwards

The Take Away

Exploring Cobá's jungly ruins was magical, and climbing Nohoch Mul really was a high. But more than anything, I was delighted to be standing on the brink of motherhood as I meant to go on – with adventure in my heart, and Junior along for the ride.

The Build Up

Entry to the ruins of the Mayan city of Cobá costs M$64. Buses run there from popular spots on the Yucatan peninsula's coastline: Cancun (three hours), Playa del Carmen (two hours) and Tulum (45 minutes). There are also plenty of guided tours organised by hotels and tour companies, many of which will combine a few hours' exploration of Cobá with a visit to a Mayan village and a dip in a cenote (the freshwater-filled limestone sinkholes that the Mayans believed were gateways to the underworld).

Cobá itself is a large site – it was an important city and trading hub for the Mayans, in use until the 13th century – and it's about a kilometre from the entrance to Nohoch Mul. Vehicles are not allowed inside, so wear sensible shoes or hire a cycle-rickshaw ('Mayan limo') to shortcut longer stretches. Climbing Nohoch Mul is still permitted – unlike the centrepiece pyramids at Chichén Itzá and Tulum in the same region – and Cobá's jungle-bound temples, ball courts, carvings and roadways are less manicured and more atmospheric than the sights at these more popular spots.

Left: making the ascent of Nohoch Mul, the Yucatan peninsula's tallest pyramid
Above: the region's many species of bird include the keel-billed toucan

32

© Yongyut Kumsri | Shutterstock. © Peter Adams Photography Ltd | Alamy Stock Photo. Next page: © Simon Dubreuil | 500px

AN ARCTIC PICNIC

UUMMANNAQ, GREENLAND

We were yelping and whooshing specks lost in a vast white wilderness. Our convoy of eight dog sleds was in the grasp of Greenland, travelling 70km (43 miles) across a frozen fjord half the size of Denmark. And then we stopped.

Clearly there was a purpose behind the pause, and it wasn't long before our Inuit drivers had bored a hole through the 2m-thick ice and dropped a fishing line – dotted with a hundred baited hooks – into the chilly depths. When the end of the line was secured to a stake, we journeyed on, eventually halting for the night to pitch our tents. There, beneath the never setting sun, we scoffed a supper of barbecued seal steaks.

The next morning we returned to our ice hole, gathering around expectantly like children at a lucky dip. Our haul from the depths included eight mighty halibut! Our jubilant hosts quickly boiled up chunks of ice on a primus stove and threw in some super-fresh fillets. Tipped onto a plate of snow, these Arctic treats were then devoured eagerly by simply using our fingers. Drinks were provided by icicles snapped from the summit of a stranded iceberg. This is how fast food should be, and it was one of the most glorious meals I'd ever

enjoyed. It wasn't just about the sublime taste, the far-reaching views, or the camaraderie of strangers – it was the sheer, epiphanic realisation of the unspeakable highs that the finest travel experiences can bring. As Greenland's great hero explorer, Knud Rasmussen, put it: 'Just give me dogs, give me winter, and you can forget the rest.'

By Nigel Tisdall

An Inuit guide holds one of the catch's small fries

Above: huskies take a well-earned break from their Arctic endeavours

A fast-food serving hatch, Greenland-style

The Take Away

Dog sledding is a traditional part of life in Greenland, and my time with the Inuit and their snarling huskies taught me how their resourceful and fascinating culture has been built around attuning to nature rather than trying to conquer it. It's an important lesson for the world.

The Build Up

Dog-sledding trips in Greenland range from two-hour excursions to multi-day adventures. The first might typically cost 1100Dkr per person including transfers. An eight-day expedition featuring helicopter flights and four nights' dog sledding with accommodation in a mix of guesthouses, huts and camping costs around 18,000Dkr per person including guides, meals and snowsuit. Some trips start and return to the same point, others spend nights at different locations. The more varied the experience the better – while sitting on a husky-drawn sled wrapped in furs is certainly romantic, it can also get cold, uncomfortable and monotonous after a couple of hours. Ask if there are one or two passengers per sled (single travellers may have to share) and if you need to rent a winter jacket, trousers and boots.

On the west coast, dog sledding is only available north of the Arctic Circle and March to May is the optimum time. How much daylight you get will depend on the time of year and how far north you are – more hours of darkness increase your chance of seeing the Northern Lights, but will also be colder. Dog-sledding trips and accommodation in Uummannaq can be arranged through Uummannaq Seasafaris (uummannaqseasafaris. gl); for more options contact Visit Greenland (greenland.com).

33

A wall at the Temple of the Lion, Naga

Below: the pyramids of Meroe in Sudan date back some 4600 years

DUNES, GLYPHS AND PYRAMIDS

BEGRAWIYA (MEROE), SUDAN

The warm whispering wind stirred the hair around my face as I climbed the cool dunes. Mine were the only footprints marking the landscape as I paced to the sharp, ridged crest. And with the sugary sand crunching between my toes, I waited for the first fingers of dawn to illuminate the pyramids of Meroe – the burial site of the Kushite kings and queens of the 25th Dynasty who ruled Egypt for more than a century.

Wandering among these honey-coloured chunks of nibbled-by-time Toblerone, I dipped my head to enter the tomb of Prince Arik-kharer. Rough glyphs decorated the walls. I studied them quietly then stopped dead in my tracks. I recognised the scene before me. Ten years previously, I'd seen the same spell scratched onto papyrus inside the British Museum in London. Taken from the Book of the Dead, the 'weighing of the heart' measures a mortal's soul against the feather of truth; if found to be heavier it was devoured by Ammut – a mythical creature with the head of a crocodile and the body of a lion – but if lighter they could pass into the afterlife.

The hairs on the back of my neck stood up as I ran my fingers over the ancient symbols hewn by Kushite hands more than 4600 years ago. And I knew this experience in these timeworn tombs would happily follow me until the end of my days.

By Emma Thomson

© Emma Thomson

90

Local transport is rather lively in the desert

The Take Away

No ticket turnstiles. No fences. A Unesco World Heritage Site standing unencumbered and free in the Sahara sand. I remember a jolt of pure joy at the genuine sense of discovery. It's not every day you get to feel like Indiana Jones.

The Build Up

Sudan's Royal Pyramids of Meroe are a three-hour drive northeast of Khartoum, the country's capital. Entrance costs US$25. Some guides still recommend paying in Sudanese pounds because it works out 30% cheaper, but this local payment isn't considered official and deprives the site of restoration fees.

You'll need to bring your own water and food. Climbing on these Unesco World Heritage-listed structures is forbidden.

Other than Egyptians, everyone requires a visa in order to enter Sudan, which must be obtained from an embassy prior to travel. Proof of yellow fever vaccination may be requested on arrival.

When arriving in Khartoum it is compulsory to register within three days at the Aliens Registration Office. With no tourist transportation, most travellers use a tour operator, which will register you on your behalf, otherwise you will need to take a spare passport photograph, copies of your passport and visa and a letter from a sponsor for processing. Similarly, travel and photo permits are compulsory when leaving the capital. These are issued free of charge by the Ministry of Tourism and Wildlife, but again if you are travelling with a tour operator they will be obtained for you.

LONG-AWAITED TIGER SIGHTING

BANDHAVGARH TIGER RESERVE, MADHYA PRADESH, INDIA

I was in the steamy central Indian forests of Bandhavgarh and it was the most unforgettable moment. Rewind 14 years and I had journeyed to Kanha National Park – the inspiration for Rudyard Kipling's Jungle Book. I went in search of Shere Khan, but after spending a whole week taking jeep safaris twice a day, I came away without so much as a pugmark for my efforts. Five years on and I tried again, this time in southern Nepal – three more safaris, and still no tigers.

For the first couple of hours this time around it was Kanha revisited: plenty of monkeys and deer, but no Shere Khan. Then suddenly came the growl. *A deep, thunderous growl, reverberating through the whole forest. The excitement was overwhelming. More tourist-packed jeeps joined ours and I feared the noise would scare the tiger before we'd even seen it. But slowly, and now silently, the most majestic creature I have ever laid my eyes upon emerged from the thicket, right in front of us. A fully grown tigress, padding her way out of the undergrowth and onto our dirt track. Everyone went wild – cameras snapping, voices whooping – but she didn't care. Too cool, this cat. She just kept on walking, across my path, and back into her jungle.*

By Daniel McCrohan

The Take Away

Nothing sweetens success more than the bitter taste of failure, and I certainly had my share of it before achieving my lifelong dream. Unusually, I had no camera. But I'm glad. I was the only one there who didn't take their eyes off that tiger. I soaked her up. Completely. She will never be forgotten.

The Build Up

Getting to Bandhavgarh Tiger Reserve is an adventure in itself. The nearest train station is in the small town of Umaria, which is about an hour by bus from the village of Tala, which is the park's gateway. Jeep safaris run twice a day from 1 October to 30 June, excluding Wednesdays when only the morning option is available. Safaris are best booked early, with most tickets becoming available 120 days in advance. Seventy-two (enough for 12 jeeps) are held to be sold on the day at the ticket office in Tala, but you may have to queue overnight to snag them.

The official booking website (forest.mponline.gov.in) doesn't as yet accept foreign bank cards for payment, so most foreign nationals go through a tour agency such as The Tiger Safari (thetigersafari. com), or ask their accommodation in Tala to help them. Places to stay in Tala include Nature Heritage Resort (natureheritageresort.com), Tiger's Den (tigerdenbandhavgarh. com) or, for those on a tight budget, Kum Kum Home.

Other tiger parks in India offering similar jeep-safari experiences include Kanha National Park and Pench National Park, both also in Madhya Pradesh, and Ranthambore National Park in Rajasthan.

Left: you'll find the world's highest density of Royal Bengal tigers in Bandhavgarh Tiger Reserve

35

POST-TSUNAMI VOLUNTEERING

ONAGAWA, JAPAN

On a sunny midsummer morning in July 2011, I took a motorboat across Onagawa Bay with fellow volunteers from Miyagi Prefecture's post-disaster clean-up crew. Four months had passed since the Great East Japan Earthquake and tsunami, which annihilated port towns such as Onagawa and killed more than 18,500 people. The sea was calm now, and so clear that you could see submerged kitchen knives and sake bottles washed out from tsunami-stricken houses, glinting in the shallows. We landed at Izushima, a small nearby island where the local fishing community had been engulfed by the incoming wave.

Evacuated and deserted except for stray cats, it was strewn with wreckage that we set about clearing. Like most of our duties in and around Onagawa, this was hot, tiring work, carried out in thick black mud filled with dead fish and jagged debris. There was, of course, a heavy atmosphere of grief and loss all around us. But I can also say that I was sublimely happy to be there. I'd been living on the other side of Japan at the time of the tsunami, and came east to report from the disaster zone. I stayed to help because I could.

I had never felt so at home among Japanese people as I did on that crew. A new sense of camaraderie and purpose was forged.

And when we took a swim at break time that afternoon, in cobalt blue water under thick green coastal mountains, I thought I'd never been anywhere so beautiful.

By Stephen Phelan

© Yasuyoshi Chiba | Getty, © Anadolu Agency | Getty

The Take Away

I had lived in Japan for years before the tsunami in March 2011, but I only got to know the place and its people by volunteering in Onagawa after the disaster. Cultural barriers broke down and customary politeness gave way to real warmth, in a gorgeous and relatively obscure corner of the country.

The Build Up

Regular Shinkansen train services run from Tokyo to Sendai, where local trains provide onward connections to Onagawa via Ishinomaki (¥6800). On arrival at the new landmark station, designed by award-winning architect Shigeru Ban, you'll see that reconstruction work is still very much ongoing. A whole new town centre is being developed on raised land behind the main fishing wharf, while surrounding mountains are terraced to create space for replacement housing high above the tsunami inundation line.

At time of writing, there is only one hotel in this 'new' Onagawa – the basic but friendly and comfortable El Faro (hotel-elfaro.com), near the Seapal Pier shopping precinct. Conceived as a stylish modern version of a traditional wooden Japanese village, this precinct consists of various bars and restaurants, a diving store, a gourmet coffee house, a ceramic tile factory and a workshop where electric guitars are carved from local *sugi* (cedar) trees.

These retailers and amenities make Onagawa unique in the tsunami impact zone – the town is not simply being rebuilt, but entirely remodelled to make itself more vibrant, youthful and attractive both to residents and tourists. Izushima island is also inhabited again, with regular boat services from Onagawa port. Visiting is a great way to actively help this community return to life.

Above: police and volunteers in Miyagi search through rubble after the 2011 earthquake and tsunami
Left: homes and cars destroyed by the force of the natural disaster

36

COAST PATH CONQUEST

CORNWALL, ENGLAND

Cornwall's Coast Path almost broke me on the first day. Within minutes of setting out from Bude on a hazy June morning, the spring in my step was being squashed by my 16kg pack. Still. 27km to Boscastle? A mere trifle, I'd thought. At a leisurely 5km an hour, I could linger over lunch and still be there by teatime.

Little did I know. This 307km stretch of England's South West Coast Path isn't just arguably the most beautiful hiking route in the country, studded with Poldark-pretty villages, spooky derelict mines and glorious beaches. It's also a rollercoaster of a trail, its total ascent greater than the height of Everest. So it was 10 hours after departing Bude that I crawled into Boscastle's Cobweb Inn, with barely the strength to lift pint to mouth.

Yet, a week later, pain had been eclipsed by delight. With fresh pollock sizzling on my camping stove, I gazed across artsy St Ives and plotted my approach to the very toe-tip of Britain. Noon the next day found me munching a saffron bun overlooking the Gurnard's Head promontory, which juts into Atlantic waters as turquoise as the Aegean. Dorsal fins sliced through the brine: one, two, three basking sharks, gulping plankton as they cruised off shore. Where should I camp tonight, I pondered... Pendeen? Perhaps push on to Sennen? Detour inland to find Neolithic dolmens or barrows?

And there it was – the sudden flash of realisation: these two legs, so frangible seven days earlier, could carry me to almost anywhere in the world.

By Paul Bloomfield

The Take Away

That coastal trek brought jaw-dropping views – but more importantly it offered a glimpse of real freedom. With boots on my feet, I could change direction on a whim, turn left or right, not restricted by car parks or train timetables or hotel bookings. Walking is travel at its purest.

The Build Up

The South West Coast Path is, until the completion of the full England Coast Path mooted for 2020, Britain's longest national trail. Snaking 1014km (630 miles) around England's southernmost limb, from

Minehead in Somerset to South Haven Point near Poole in Dorset, it traverses the entire coastline of Devon and Cornwall. Typical walkers take six to eight weeks to complete the whole trail, though many tackle it in shorter chunks; the Cornwall Coast Path, covering 307km (191 miles) between Bude and Falmouth, is among the most challenging (and beautiful) sections, taking two or three weeks to walk.

Campsites are plentiful along this stretch, though not ubiquitous – in some places B&Bs or hotels are the only options, so some hikers wild-camp (which is, strictly speaking, illegal). Campsites get booked out

in July and August, but many have a hikers-only area that usually has walk-up availability. Several tour operators offer guided or supported hikes on various sections.

The path involves several ferry crossings of rivers or harbours, some of which operate infrequently or on limited dates. Also, the Dorset stretch crosses the restricted military area called Lulworth Ranges, open only on limited days; check details in advance.

Left: the sun sets over Land's End in Cornwall, at England's western tip

37

RIDING THE MIDNIGHT TRAIN

URGENCH TO TASHKENT, UZBEKISTAN

Uncomfortable, I drifted between sleep and vigilance, kept in a transient state by the rhythm of the train. I was riding on the overnight service from Urgench to Tashkent, and found myself squeezed into the top bunk of an open couchette car.

From my perch I could hear the rustles of people walking back and forth below me, and at an early stop I looked out through the open window to the platform, observing merchants hawking their crispy 12-inch flatbreads. When I twisted to look inside the car, I glimpsed more surreal snapshots of Uzbek life: the intricate black braid of a girl; a group of women sat together watching – of all things – Braveheart dubbed in Russian; a couple of men in kalpoq caps sucking sugar cubes between their gold teeth.

The latter pair invited me to share tea – I watched as they carefully demonstrated the proper Uzbek pouring technique: three times in the teapot, three times in the cup, then drink. I was absorbed in process, all the while Mel Gibson's painted blue face loomed above me.

Back in my bunk I felt neither present nor far away, but somewhere in between. As the night went on the names of the stations floated past like ghosts of the Silk Road: Navoiy, Jizzakh, Gulistan. The desert air blew into my face, brisk and smelling of the sun. From my vantage point, as the light started to return to the landscape, I watched, enthralled, the undulation of the desert dunes outside.

By Wailana Kalama

The Take Away

When I look back, I'm filled with a sense of calm. I'd always been a tense traveller, constantly worrying about what came next. But that night, I was free from anxiety. I was simply absorbing the myriad sights without analysing them. For the first time in my travels, I felt serene.

The Build Up

The overnight train from Urgench to Tashkent departs daily at 2.40pm and arrives at 7.10am the following day. Check the schedule and ticket prices on the Uzbek Railways website (uzrailpass.uz). Night trains travel at a slower speed (90kmh/56mph) than their daylight counterparts, with more stopovers on the road, including Bukhara, Nukus, Termez and other towns.

The least expensive bed is in an open couchette car (*platzkart* carriage), but for more private spaces there's the four-berth wagon (*kupe* carriage) and the two-berth wagon (*spalniy vagon*) compartment.

The easiest way to buy tickets is in advance at the train station, but you can also purchase them at Real Russia (realrussia.co.uk/trains/tickets) at a considerable markup. Note that trains to Tashkent tend to sell out quickly, especially in the peak months of July and August, so buy at least a few days in advance.

The main international gateway to Uzbekistan is Tashkent, which is linked to Istanbul, Moscow and other European and Asian cities by various airlines, including Uzbekistan Airways (uzairways.com). Visas are required prior to travel, but they are relatively painless to obtain, and most nationalities no longer require a letter of invitation.

Left: the train ploughs through the Uzbek countryside for more than 700km
Below: passengers having a gander from the Urgench to Tashkent train

38

FLOATING AMONG GIANTS ON CANOE SAFARI

LOWER ZAMBEZI NATIONAL PARK, ZAMBIA

With each stroke of the paddle I knew I was stirring a river where giants lurk. As I glided slowly along the still surface of the Zambezi in my canoe, I quickly got the feeling that I was being watched. Eyes popped up here and there, vanishing beneath the surface as swiftly as they appeared. I listened to my guide in the boat ahead and stuck to the shallows, which in theory should keep the onlookers at a distance, something you're grateful for given these eyes belong to creatures that weigh over 1500kg and can sport canines that are half a metre long. Hippos are much like icebergs – what looms below is far more impressive than what is visible above the water and, most importantly, you never want to crash into one.

The mighty river's banks were no less dramatic – vervet monkeys screeched from branches to warn of prowling leopards, hulking elephants towered over the sandbanks, and 5m-long Nile crocodiles basked in the sun with their mouths agape and their glistening teeth on display. I even spent some time following a lion pride that was patrolling the water's edge just a few metres away. When they stopped to slake their thirst, I looked each of them in the eye. As intimate as it was alarming, the lion encounter was much like the

paddle itself – an intoxicating mix of emotions, spliced with glorious sights and sounds.

By Aurelia India Birwood

The Take Away

Despite the natural theatrics and sense of danger, the experience was full of peace and absolute wonder. I was witnessing the world's most iconic species of wildlife living their unique lives on their terms. I was a guest in a world that was not mine. And it's impossible to ever forget that.

The Take Away

The Zambezi River marks the entire southern boundary of Zambia's Lower Zambezi National Park, and most of the lodges and camps within the area operate canoe safaris along it. Some choose to stick to the main channel, while others skirt along the minor channels within the depths of the bush. Depending on your level of paddling experience, you may be in your own boat with another capable guest, or be paired with one of the guides.

Walking safaris are also possible in the park with your lodge's guides and armed park rangers, and – like canoe options – provide a more intimate experience with the wildlife, both large and small. Without the rumble of a 4WD engine, and without the protective feeling of being in a large vehicle, your senses are heightened to each and every sound and movement in the nearby bush. One moment you'll be crouching down to wait out nearby buffalo, while in another you'll be doubled over to examine the fascinating traps laid by antlions.

Getting to Lower Zambezi National Park is as easy as a 30-minute flight from Zambia's capital, Lusaka (proflight-zambia.com).

Above: as serene as surreal, a sunset paddle along the Zambezi River, with an elephant for company
Left: when canoeing the Zambezi, some obstacles require a wider berth than others

39

HITTING NEW HIMALAYAN HIGHS

NAMCHE BAZAAR, NEPAL

It was 4.40am in the village of Namche Bazaar, Nepal. Through my window, the jagged edges of Thamserku (6623m) were backlit by the moon. Unable to sleep, I walked into the dawn. Even at this hour, the capital of the Himalayan Khumbu region would normally have been bustling. But six months earlier, two earthquakes rocked Nepal, leaving 9000 people dead and the country saddled with US$5 billion in damages. As a result, tourism had stopped and Namche Bazaar was a ghost town.

It had been an emotional few weeks of travelling. In Kathmandu, I saw ancient temples reduced to piles of rubble and entire rural villages relocated to makeshift tarp cities. Yesterday, my friend Mingma Dorji Sherpa and I trekked a half-day west of Namche Bazaar to the village of Thame, where 90% of the houses had been destroyed, to check in on some of Mingma's elderly relatives. When we arrived, Mingma's aunt and uncle were sitting outside an International Red Cross tent. Tears ran down their faces when they recognised their nephew from Kathmandu. A few steps away, their new home, rebuilt by neighbours, would soon be ready to inhabit.

That morning, as I watched the sun rise over the peaks cradling Namche Bazaar, I thought about the back-breaking efforts every Nepali I met had put forth to rebuild their country. It flooded me with a deep sense of respect followed by the rush of joy that hope brings. If any country can survive an earthquake, I thought, this one can.

By Stephanie Pearson

The Take Away

My most transformative travel moments never have anything to do with exquisite meals, fine wines and luxury hotels. The beauty of travel for me is in forming relationships with people and witnessing the challenges and joys they face even in the most difficult times.

The Build Up

The best time of year to trek in the Khumbu is spring and autumn. All independent foreign trekkers in Nepal are required to carry a Trekkers Information Management Systems (TIMS) card (Rs2000) available from government-registered trekking offices in Kathmandu. Because Namche Bazaar and the surrounding Himalayan peaks such as Mount Everest are located in Sagarmatha National Park, trekkers must also pay a park entry fee (Rs3390), also obtainable in Kathmandu at the Tourist Service Centre. For more information on both the card and the park entry fee, visit welcomenepal.com.

Most trekkers to Namche Bazaar and beyond begin in Lukla, a 45-minute flight from Kathmandu, world-renowned for its airport runway that sits at 2860m (9380ft) and drops off the side of a cliff. From Lukla, Namche Bazaar is only 13.5km (8 miles) and sits 580m (1900ft) higher. The short distance is misleading. At altitudes this high, trekkers need to be careful to acclimatise slowly. In Namche Bazaar, guest houses are plentiful and cost roughly Rs2500 per night. Because of the altitude, variable weather, and the logistics of acquiring permits and lodging, many trekkers sign up with a reputable guiding company like REI.com/adventures.

Left: the 6623m (21,680ft) peak of Mt Thamserku in Nepal
Above: the Nepalese people have showed great resilience since the 2015 earthquake

PETRA BY CANDLELIGHT

PETRA, JORDAN

What brought me to Jordan wasn't its impressively Biblical ruins, ephemeral golden sands or the Lawrence of Arabia romance of Wadi Rum. It was a childhood glimpse of the rose-red lost city of the Nabataeans in a well-thumbed copy of Hergé's The Adventures of Tintin. The Treasury, Petra's most exhilarating rock temple, made a lasting impression that has stuck for a lifetime.

So when standing stock-still at its base, my childlike wonder was uncontainable. It was born from the dusty pillars, the splintered canyon chipped away by the millennia, the horses riding out to the sandstone crypt, framed by golden cliffs fading to shadow.

When my eyes caught sight of the Bedouin, who were swaddled in cowls and flame-red keffiyehs, the intense feeling of nostalgia was instantly replaced by one of pure elation. As if ghosts, they glided out from the Siq passageway in a ceremonial procession, holding flickering candles aloft. Somehow, their sparkling eyes seemed to stare deep into my soul.

Over the next hour, as the night sky grew in confidence, I watched as a thousand torches sparked life into this gateway to the underworld. It came in ever-variegated stages, a dusky orange afterglow at first, followed by a pink glimmer, and finally a smoky purple cast across the rock face, a blanket of stars unfolding above.

The Bedouin took turns to sing wistful desert laments, while I embraced the scene's timeless melancholy. The world turns on moments like this, I thought. And if an ancient Nabataean deity had appeared from the shadows to carry away my soul, I would have gladly followed.

By Mike MacEacheran

The Take Away

Modern life encourages us to value borders – and yet Petra is a time warp of cultural interactions as beguiling today as it would have been a thousand years ago. I shiver when I recall that night, but I take it to mean so much more: if there is hope and possibility, it lies in such a place.

The Build Up

Entry tickets to Petra (JD50) are available from the Visitor Centre, only moments away from the village of Wadi Musa (visitpetra. jo). Considering the archaeological site's monstrous scale, many visitors opt to buy a two- or three-day ticket (JD55–60).

Petra can get mind-bogglingly busy during the peak season (March to May and September to November), particularly so after 10am when the tour buses from Aqaba to the south and the Dead Sea resorts to the north begin to offload.

To achieve a soul-stirring adrenaline rush, you can avoid the crush by arriving before sunrise, or when Petra basks in golden hour sunlight (the site opens between 6am and 6pm in summer, closing at 4pm in winter).

To see Petra bathed in candlelight (Monday, Wednesday and Thursday; JD17), your journey will begin at 8.30pm when those-in-the-know gather at the Visitor Centre for the torch-lit, 1km walk down the Siq canyon. Returning back at 10.30pm, you'll forever be haunted by the language, symbolism and optimism of such a magical night out.

Left: candles illuminate the Siq – the passageway to the ancient city of Petra

41

A BROTHERHOOD ON KILI

MT KILIMANJARO, TANZANIA

As the realisation sunk in that we had reached the roof of Africa and were now standing in the same spot our dad did some four decades earlier, my throat constricted and I felt the prickle of tears beginning to well up in my eyes. Coming together from three different continents to follow in the footsteps of our father had been more than a year in the planning. And the route to the summit involved some tribulations too – sleepless nights in the tents, brotherly bickering and many aches and pains – yet all this faded away as my two brothers and I hugged one another almost 6000m above sea level.

Over the seven previous days on the Machame route, we had ascended through diverse landscapes: rainforest with its chattering monkeys and colourful flora; alpine zones covered in alien scrub and palm-like lobelia; energy-sapping scree fields, which appeared almost lunar in their make-up; and finally, up at Uhuru Peak (5895m) on Kibo Crater's edges, thin air, extreme temperatures and glaciers.

Earlier that day, climbing up the eastern ridge to the summit in the pitch black night, we'd paused to take in the sunrise as day broke and Mawenzi Peak was silhouetted perfectly against a backdrop of orange, pink and blue hues. A day of delights to be sure, and best of all, one inspired by our dad.

By David Gorvett

Above: the summit calls to all those hoping to reach the top of Africa **Below**: thick ice in equatorial Africa says everything about Kilimanjaro's lofty status

The Take Away

It isn't the memories of beautiful views, or the sense of accomplishment that I treasure the most, but the shared experience – it was a bond forged with my brothers that we won't forget. It's also the consolidation of a tradition my four-year-old nephew has already vowed to uphold.

The Build Up

Treks depart all year, but the best times (in order to avoid the rains) are between late June and October, and from late December to February. The two key centres for organising treks are the nearby cities of Moshi and Arusha, both of which are serviced by Kilimanjaro International Airport.

Kilimanjaro can only be climbed with a licensed guide, and it's recommended to organise your climb through a tour company. No-frills four-night/five-day treks up the Marangu Route start at about US$1500, including park fees and taxes, and no-frills six-day budget treks on the Machame Route start at around US$1900. Prices start at about US$1500 on the Rongai Route, and about US$2000 for a seven-day trek on the Shira Plateau Route.

The better companies provide dining tents, decent-to-good cuisine and various other extras to make the experience more enjoyable and maximise your chances of getting to the top. To further increase your chances of success, seriously consider adding at least one extra day onto the 'standard' climb itineraries.

42

STARING INTO
AN ACTIVE VOLCANO

ASO-KUJU NATIONAL PARK, KYUSHU, JAPAN

I anxiously held my breath as the helicopter's blades pulled us skywards. The sensation was unlike anything I had ever experienced, and it crossed my mind that this was the nearest thing to the inexplicable feeling of freedom when flying in one's dreams. We were at altitude in what seemed like the blink of an eye and my fear slowly subsided, allowing me to relax into my seat and start to take in the surroundings. We were floating gracefully above the landscape and the strong afternoon sun was casting the shadow of the helicopter over the luscious green expanse of trees surrounding the national park.

As the foliage gave away to a sloping, rocky incline, we rose higher towards the toothy crater of Mt Aso, Japan's largest active volcano. As a photographer, I am always eager to see the world from a different angle, and this one was truly striking.

I clutched my camera, eager to capture the contents of the great leviathan. Without saying a word, our pilot manoeuvred the craft over the opening of the crater and I gazed in wonder at the bubbling lake below. We hovered for a few moments, allowing me to quickly

snap some shots, before we circled the entire crater's edge. Later, as the pilot brought us down with expert precision, I exhaled, feeling a mixture of relief, excitement and wonder.

By James Gabriel Martin

Look but don't touch when sitting next to the pilot

© James Gabriel Martin

Mt Aso is the biggest active volcano in Japan

The Take Away

The exhilarating mix of emotions that surged through me at take-off (and landing) is something that will stay with me forever. The experience taught me a valuable lesson: sometimes life's greatest moments come when we leave our comfort zone and step into scary, unchartered territory.

The Build Up

The volcanic caldera of Mt Aso (known affectionately as Aso-san throughout Japan) consists of five peaks that stand in Aso-Kuju National Park, which is located between Kumamoto and Beppu on Kyushu, Japan's third-largest island. Helicopter rides are operated by a selection of tour companies, including Saga Aviation (sgc-air. co.jp), which offers different price options according to flight time. Experiences range from a two-minute flight over the pastures at the foot of one of the peaks (¥3000), to a 10 minute jaunt over the centre of the active Nakadake crater (¥13,000). Other companies (insidejapantours.com) offer helicopter experiences as part of package deals that include a five-night stay, transportation and guided excursions.

The area is active geologically, and Mt Aso had a major eruption as recently as 2016. Large-scale earthquakes also affect the region and can lead to closures of roads, which can occasionally limit access to hiking routes. However, frequently updated information on access routes can be found at the Aso website (aso.ne.jp/~volcano/eng).

Above: any anxiety about the copter ride dissipated with a close-up perspective of Mt Aso's crater

43

CYCLING THE TEMPLE TRAIL

SIEM REAP, CAMBODIA

The sweltering heat oozed off the tarmac as I followed my guide Samnang down a dirt track and into the welcome respite of the shade. 'This way,' he said. I was cycling to Beng Mealea, the ancient temple believed to be the basis of the majestic Angkor Wat. Despite it being 68km (42 miles) from Siem Reap, Samnang still wanted to take the longer scenic route. There were things he needed to show me, he said.

I followed him into a quiet village, where the crackle of our tyres on gravel heralded the arrival of a dozen young children running. Their joy was infectious as they followed in our dusty wake. As we cycled away, their innocent shouts rang in my ears. The world here felt simpler, happier.

We pushed on, past paddy fields, through lush landscapes. A UN Land Rover was parked by the roadside, four uniformed men carefully combing an empty field. 'They're training to find land mines,' said Samnang. The innocence of earlier was swiftly replaced by the realisation that in Cambodia, the past is always close at hand.

Planting mines in ancient temples was one of the Khmer Rouge's final insults. 'Beng Mealea was only cleared in 2007,' explained Samnang as we arrived.

Together we slowly explored the dazzling warren of crumbling temples, overrun by knotted trees and vines. All the while, I looked around in awe, breathed in the cool air of the forest and bathed in the site's majesty and the region's long history.

By Joe Minihane

© Sasin Tipchai | 500px, © Dale Johnson | 500px

The Take Away

Cycling with Samnang helped me to realise how Cambodia's 20th-century conflict was inextricably linked with its ancient past. Until then, the history of this place felt abstract. That day continues to serve as a vital reminder that nothing can beat learning from the locals.

The Take Away

Day tours by bicycle to the temples around Siem Reap are available from a number of different operators in the province, including Grasshopper Adventures (grasshopperadventures.com). Prices start from US$45, with trips including water, snacks, lunch and bikes, as well as support from a tuk-tuk, which carries extra supplies.

Rides typically start early (about 7am) in an attempt to beat the heat, which can become stifling, especially between December and March. Experience of cycling longer distances is recommended, as the ride can become tough as the sun beats down. It is possible to take breaks and ride in the tuk-tuk if the heat becomes too much.

Beng Mealea is not as popular as the temples of Angkor, meaning there are fewer tourists and greater scope to explore. Visitors should stick to dedicated paths, however, and avoid climbing on the ruins. Admission to Beng Mealea (US$5) is not included in the Angkor Wat pass (US$37 for one day, or US$62 for three days), which covers most temples around Siem Reap.

Half-day rides to Angkor Wat are also available for those who want to pedal to the temples but don't fancy a strenuous workout.

Above: trees have taken root in the ruins of the ancient temple of Beng Mealea
Left: an improvised parasol in the Cambodian fields

44

GOOD HEAVENS ABOVE

MAKGADIKGADI PANS, BOTSWANA

Donning cloth turbans, we sped on our quad bikes, single file, into the empty void of the salt pans – Mad Max meets Lawrence of Arabia. It was hard to imagine, two million years ago, this was Africa's largest lake, the size of Victoria and Tanganyika lakes combined. Earlier in the day, we had stood in awe of its dust devils, mirages and searing whiteness, but night cast a different kind of spell. Steely starlight bathed the pans in an ethereal glow. After 30km (19 miles), we stopped. The silence was sudden, intense.

'Walk out there, lie on your back and enjoy,' our guide told us. There was nothing to aim for, so I paced a hundred steps. Turning slowly full circle, I traced the uncluttered curve of the earth, a land scraped of all life, contour and landmark. I felt like an ant flicked into an ice rink. Stretching out on the salt crust, I watched a satellite drift from the west, voyaging across the glittering arch of the Milky Way until it disappeared, snuffed out by the black horizon. Scorpio unfurled its tail to the east, while the pointers, two of the nearest suns to our solar system, guided me to the Southern Cross.

An hour passed, perhaps two. It was only when a salvo of shooting stars flared overhead and I gasped, shockingly loud in the desert silence, that the spell was broken. I stood and walked slowly back to the quad bikes, drugged by stargazing, humbled by the cosmos.

By Sally Gray

The Take Away

There are few places so totally removed from the noise, pollution and clutter of modern life than Botswana's Makgadikgadi Pans. To lie down in this pristine wilderness beneath a star-spangled ceiling not only revealed how complex and beautiful our universe is, but also reminded me of my place in it.

The Build Up

Gateway to the Okavango Delta, the town of Maun is also the starting point for safaris to the Makgadikgadi Pans. Several operators offer mobile camping safaris, including Afro Trek (afrotrek.com) and Bush Ways Safaris (bushways.com).

If you're considering going it alone, venturing into Makgadikgadi away from the few main roads in the area, you will need at least two 4WD vehicles, GPS, compass and enough fuel, food and water to cope with emergencies. You can catch a bus or drive yourself (a 2WD vehicle is fine during the dry season April–October) to Gweta, a village about 200km (125 miles) from Maun that's a convenient staging post for exploring the pans. It has a rest camp, food store and restaurant, but many travellers head to Planet Baobab (unchartedafrica. com) 5km east of Gweta, where traditional Bakalanga huts (with en suite bathrooms) provide more affordable accommodation. It also offers guided activities such as quad bike expeditions, walking safaris and meerkat encounters.

More upmarket options include Camp Kalahari and Jack's Camp. Charter companies such as Kavango Air (kavangoair.com) operate light-aircraft flights between Maun and the various camps on the edge of the Makgadikgadi Pans.

Left: quad bikes provide access to the desert pans and stunning perspectives on the night sky

45

JOURNEY TO THE CENTRE OF THE EARTH

THRIHNUKAGIGUR, ICELAND

After clambering over luminescent moss-laden lava rocks that concealed treacherous underground rivers and mini waterfalls, my small group reached the business end of the dormant volcano Thrihnukagigur. As one of the first to be lowered 120m (390ft) into the belly of this natural beast, I was bursting with anticipation and excitement as I struggled to clip into the required safety gear. I then shuffled close to the edge of the volcano's surprisingly small opening (more like that of a well), and nervously walked the ridiculously narrow gangplank that was suspended above the gaping shaft. Five souls then joined me in a window-washing-type platform for our descent towards the centre of the Earth.

With the smallest of jerks, we began to drop. Soon the size of the shaft exploded outwards as we burst into the crater proper. What I did not expect, however, was an immediate outbreak of colour – the glistening walls, wet with meltwater, blazed with brilliant oranges and yellows. I felt as if I was dropping into a Picasso painting.

By the time I reached the floor I was giddy. Millions of years of history was displayed on these walls, from failed eruptions to disruptions in the planet's formation – it was all here before me and I would have only 20 minutes to drink it all in. And then I looked up at the only way out, the tiny eye in the crater's ceiling peering down at me from above.

By Chris Zeiher

© Sergii Mikushev | 500px

The Take Away

Later, as I sat quietly sharing my mutton stew with the base camp's adopted Arctic fox, I realised it wasn't just the wild beauty that overwhelmed me – it was the sheer magnitude of Thrihnukagigur's scale and history. I've never felt so small and vulnerable, yet so undeniably connected to the power of our precious planet.

The Build Up

Thrihnukagigur is just an hour outside Reykjavik in southwest Iceland, making it easily accessible from the capital. Pre-booking the Inside the Volcano experience is highly advisable (kr42,000; insidethevolcano.com). For safety reasons, access to the dormant volcano is only available in warmer months, namely between mid-May and mid-October. Tours are restricted to those 12 years old and older, though exceptions have been known.

On the day of your descent you'll either be collected from your Reykjavik hotel or, alternatively, you can meet the team at the Bláfjöll parking lot, which is the starting point for the trek across the mossy landscape.

The whole round-trip experience from Reykjavik takes approximately five to six hours and it's essential to wear good walking shoes or hiking boots for the 50-minute trek to and from base camp. And remember to dress warmly for changing weather conditions – it may be summer, but it's still Iceland! Once inside the crater itself, you'll experience stable temperatures of around 5°C.

It's important to remember that whatever you bring into the park you'll need to carry out, so travel lightly.

Left: the kaleidoscopic interior of dormant volcano Thrihnukagigur
Above: the surface, and daylight, seems a long distance away

46

FOLLOWING FINN ON THE MISSISSIPPI

MISSISSIPPI, USA

Stirring the early morning waters of the Mississippi

The wooden canoe sliced through the water, propelling us along the mighty Mississippi. Darkness slowly turned to light as the sun rose above the horizon. There wasn't another soul in sight, and no sound save for the gentle swish of the paddles.

An eagle soared overhead as my guide and I pulled up onto a sandbar – a tiny, ephemeral island that might only have emerged that morning, and in all probability would be washed away just a few hours later. I walked alongside prints left by a sizeable bird, the surface of the sand cracking underneath my bare feet, and then waded into the blissfully warm water until I was waist deep.

I'd been drawn to the Mississippi River since reading The Adventures of Huckleberry Finn as a child. In Mark Twain's book, the river becomes a symbol of freedom, and I'd long fantasised about finding that feeling while drifting along this waterway like Huck and Jim – though preferably without quite so much peril.

As I submerged myself, the exhaustion of a late night and early start slipped away, and an overwhelming sense of peace washed over me. As a city-dweller, I very rarely find true isolation or total silence, but here I'd found it in – and on – this river I'd thought about for so long.

By Nicola Trup

A bald eagle searching the river for an easy meal

The Take Away

I don't think I've ever felt as relaxed as I did that day; we paddled for 29km (18 miles) over several hours, but it felt like minutes. The sound of the paddles, and the feeling I had just being in the presence of the river, are memories I still come back to during stressful moments.

The Build Up

The Mississippi River runs through or borders 10 US states, with various canoe and kayak outfits along its length. In Mississippi, these include three outposts of Quapaw Canoe Company (island63.com); from its Clarksdale branch you can access a very quiet stretch of the river. Renting a two-person canoe costs from $35 a day, while guided excursions start at $175 per person, per day.

If you're planning to go it alone, it's best to set off around sunrise – this is when the river is at its most peaceful, and you're unlikely to encounter anyone else on the water. Plus, it allows you a few hours' paddling before the midday sun kicks in.

The Mississippi River can be very dangerous for swimmers, with hidden currents and whirlpools. However, a guide can show you the safe spots – these tend to be in the back channels and the shallows along the larger sandbars.

Similar paddling experiences can be had elsewhere in Mississippi, including the picturesque Bogue Chitto River and Black Creek, though these are more popular, so avoid weekends and public holidays if you're seeking solitude.

Below: dawn breaks over one of the Mississippi's ephemeral islands

47

EXPLORING COLOMBIA'S 'LOST CITY'

CIUDAD PERDIDA, COLOMBIA

'Don't bother,' chuckled my guide Miguel as I bent down to untie my shoes at the edge of the rushing stream. I'd soon realise that, on this hike, there was no use trying to stay dry.

Off-limits for years following narcoterrorist activity in the region, the hiking route to Ciudad Perdida, Colombia's famed 'Lost City', had recently reopened, and I couldn't resist the challenge. Following a three-day slog through the stunning but unforgiving jungle and equally unrelenting rain, we finally made it to the edge of the historical site known to local tribes as Teyuna. Ascending an ancient, moss-covered stone staircase, circular terraces began to fan out from either side like huge shelves of coral. Some were scattered with ancient artefacts – such as huge boulders engraved with maps – abandoned for centuries before being 'rediscovered' by treasure hunters in 1972. It was utterly unique compared with any other ancient ruin I'd ever seen.

Its wooden structures long-since rotted away, Ciudad Perdida isn't as visually striking as the more famous ruins of Machu Picchu or Tikal, but, for me, standing on the summit of this mysterious, ancient place hidden in the tropical jungle – which was free of touts, crowds, or a mere shred of tourism infrastructure (unless you count the Colombian military outpost) – was far more powerful. In that moment, I savoured that rare, delicious taste of pure, raw adventure.

By Sarah Reid

The Take Away

While it's always a great rush to visit travel icons you've seen captured with a thousand different Instagram filters, this experience reminded me that seeking out the world's lesser-known wonders can sometimes be far more rewarding.

The Build Up

The 44km (27 mile) round-trip to Ciudad Perdida is typically completed in four days. A guide is essential (independent hiking is not allowed), and tours are easily booked in the nearby tourist centres of Santa Marta and Taganga. Expect to pay around US$300, which includes food and basic accommodation (hammocks or bunks in open-sided shelters) en route. The December to March dry season is the most popular time to undertake the trip, though rain is possible at any time of the year.

On the first morning of the tour, you'll take a two-hour jeep ride from Santa Marta or Taganga to the small village of El Mamey, where you'll have lunch and set off for about five hours of hiking along a primitive jungle track to the first camp. Day two is a nine-hour slog to Paraiso Camp, near the foot of the staircase to the ruins (which sit at around 1100m/3600ft), with swim stops along the way. On day three, groups rise early to explore the ruins before backtracking down the route for about 9km (5½ miles) before arriving back in El Mamey on the afternoon of day four. You'll need to carry everything you'll need – operators advise to pack as light as possible for the challenging, but unforgettable, trip.

Above: Colombia's Ciudad Perdida is believed to pre-date the more famous Machu Picchu
Left: stone stairs to the city were uncovered by local treasure hunters in 1972

48

EXPLORING PRECIOUS MADAGASCAN FORESTS

ANJOZOROBE-ANGAVO FOREST CORRIDOR, MADAGASCAR

I had never heard an indri's song before. It was as soulful as a husky's howl and as abstract and mystical as whale song. I thrilled at every note.

The forest hung in dense, dewy folds around me. Somewhere deep in the shadows, the melody was becoming a chorus. I had travelled to Madagascar in the hope of seeing lemurs, and we were on the right track. All we had to do was dive into the tangle of trees and perhaps I'd catch a glimpse of something black-and-white, bounding from branch to branch.

The Anjozorobe-Angavo Forest Corridor, an extensive natural forest in Madagascar's central highlands, is one of the last strongholds of the indri, the largest living lemur. Its mighty tropical hardwoods are hemmed in by rice fields, pine plantations and villages. As we arrived, shortly after dawn, we heard a different kind of music – young farmers singing to each other in the valley below.

Is it a tune you know?' I asked Toussaint and Sesen, my guides.

'It's just a pop song,' said Sesen. 'They're playing with the harmonies.' To my ears, it was as perfect as a madrigal.

Fresh-smelling foliage brushed our shoulders as we hiked. I knew every tree could conceal something fascinating, from swivel-eyed chameleons to sleeping mouse lemurs and tiny frogs, but we pressed on.

When at last Toussaint indicated we should leave the path and fight our way uphill through knotted vines, I didn't hesitate. We were about to encounter the indris. And it would be wonderful.

By Emma Gregg

The natural treasure of this forest corridor now has protected status

The Take Away

I explored with two local guides, two generations apart, and an interpreter from Antananarivo. I wouldn't have done it any other way. I realised Madagascar's increasingly rare forests and its astonishing wildlife are in their hands, and we need to do everything in our power to help them safeguard these natural treasures.

The Build Up

The most comfortable base in Madagascar's Anjozorobe-Angavo Forest Corridor is Saha Forest Camp (sahaforestcamp.mg). This Fair Trade Tourism-certified, community-owned lodge was set up by Fanamby, a respected Madagascan conservation and development association, to enable the rural community to earn a sustainable income from forest ecotourism. Staffed by locals, it offers simple but comfortable accommodation in 10 cabins overlooking the forest. There are even better forest views from the huge deck, which has polished timber floors and comfortable sofas. Delicious, freshly cooked meals are served on the deck on request.

Local guides offer walks at very reasonable rates (Ar25,000–Ar50,000), ranging from short nocturnal wildlife-watching forays to all-day excursions, exploring the forest and visiting villages and rice plantations. For the most fulfilling experience, it's a good idea to travel to Saha with an interpreter/guide to translate, since the locals know the forest well but are not very fluent in English or French.

Saha Forest Camp is about two hours' drive from Antananarivo. Although most of the route follows well-maintained roads, a 4WD is essential after heavy rain. Guests park at a nearby hamlet and make their final approach on foot, a pleasant walk of 20-30 minutes along rice-planters' paths.

Above: the sun's rays cut through the canopy of the Madagascan forest

49

LIGHTENING THE LOAD

DHARAMKOT, INDIA

Bzzzzzd...
My heart pounds with each passing of the blade.
Bzzzzzzd...
It's a sunny day in May and I can see the Himalayas towering in front of me.
Schwomp.
This is really happening!
Swoosh!
Brown locks pass through my fingers and onto the floor.
I'm in a quaint Buddhist community just north of Dharamsala, spending time to get to know 'the real me' and... apparently, to shave my head. Travelling solo throughout Asia has indeed become my medium of self-discovery.

I look down to what can only be likened to a baby wookiee growing at my feet. It's amazing what a year-long journey after quitting your job can bring you. In my case, a complete and utter shedding.

To shave my head had been a secret desire for years, but it was always a wild wish, something I couldn't possibly do. Fear, a constant companion, had long inhibited risks and often actions – walking away from the life I knew inspired me to start standing up to them. With practice, it became easier to confront my other worries, such as the judgment of others.

Tibetan bells ring, the smell of Nag Champa fills the air as prayer flags sway overhead. Buzzing clippers in hand, I take the blade to the centre of my forehead.

With each challenge, encounter and emotional bump in the road, I let go mentally and spiritually, trusting more in myself and the world around me. And now I'm letting go physically. This is the most powerful I have ever felt.

By Ashley Garver

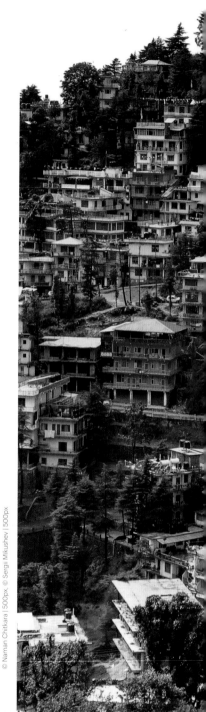

The Take Away

Travelling is empowering. It strengthens your courage muscle, while at the same time softening your ego. You learn to surrender to happenstance and learn from little moments of connection. When I began 'the shave' I was in sync with what my heart most desired from this journey – another layer of letting go.

The Build Up

Dharamsala (or Dharamshala) is a city in the state of Himachal Pradesh and is most well known for being the home of the Dalai Lama and Central Tibetan Administration (aka the Tibetan Government in Exile).

From Delhi, you can get there by plane, train (via Pathankot) or bus, the latter taking about 12 hours. The bus station is in the southern end of town known as Lower Dharamsala, while it is Upper Dharamsala, namely an area called Mcloed Ganj, where his holiness resides.

A 15-minute walk further north you'll reach Dharamkot, a relaxed village surrounded by cedar forest on the outskirts of the Himalayas. There you will find a number of yoga and meditation centres and you can sign up to take classes in a variety of healing methodologies from crystals to Ayurveda. This village is a great hub for hikes to surrounding vistas, waterfalls and monasteries.

People tend to stay in Dharamkot for weeks and even months at a time, and thus it has a strong community vibe. Barbers can be found in every town big or small in India. If you're looking for that empowering feeling, ask around, your fellow travellers might have some clippers.

Left: the colourful hillside town of Dharamsala
Above: Tibetan bells ring out in the nearby
Buddhist community of Dharamkot

DISCOVERING ANCIENT PERSIA

KHARANAQ, IRAN

The ancient dwellings form a wondrous labyrinth

We pulled off the desert highway and drove through the abandoned streets of a small, seemingly ordinary town. Then, after rounding a corner, there it was – the 1000-year-old village of Kharanaq, perched serenely as if it too was contemplating its history. Standing before me was an imposing citadel wall, and stretching down towards a green valley were the rounded tops of decaying mud-brick houses.

Chickens pecked around my feet as I exited the car and headed towards a tall, arched entrance. As the path narrowed it soon became apparent that I was following my guide into a labyrinth of ancient alleyways and tunnels. Ducking my head I entered tiny rooms and carefully negotiated crumbling steps up into yet smaller rooms. As I noticed thick black soot – remnants of ancient fires – staining the ceiling of one claustrophobic room, I wondered about the families who would have made these minuscule dwellings their homes. Looking down I spotted a piece of broken pottery, its dark green glaze still shiny under the dust. How old could it be?

I was so lost in moments like these – each incredibly still and peaceful – that it wasn't until I stopped to gaze over the valley that I realised I had been wandering, climbing and exploring on my own. I had not encountered a single soul. I felt privileged to be there, and staggered that such places as Kharanaq can still be virtually undiscovered.

By Claire Beyer

The Take Away

It was truly incredible to have such a piece of Persian history all to myself in that moment. It felt as if I was the one to discover the cultural treasures of Kharanaq for the very first time. Negative preconceptions make Iran almost devoid of tourists, which in an increasingly travelled world is a unique thing to experience in itself.

The Build Up

Kharanaq is easily accessible on a day trip from the enchanting desert town of Yazd, some 70km (43 miles) to the south. The hour-long drive will take you along the fringes of the barren but impressive Dasht-e Lut desert until you reach the hilly green pocket in which the village nestles. While organised tours are an option, most hotels in Yazd can arrange a taxi here, which means that you don't have to commit to specific times. Visiting in the afternoon means you can wander down into the valley to an ancient aqueduct and watch the village above change hue as the sun sets.

The highlight of your visit will be getting lost among the winding alleys, so make sure you have given yourself enough time to explore the place and enjoy the solitude. The best time to visit is either in spring or in autumn as summer temperatures can be uncomfortably hot. Yazd is well connected to other cities in the region by air, bus and some train services.

Below: the mud-brick houses of kharanaq are around 1000 years old

51

THE PARIS OPERA
IN THE DESERT

SAHARA DESERT, MOROCCO

In a moment of inexplicable madness, I decided to take part in the Marathon des Sables, a seven-day, 250km-long pain-fest in the Sahara Desert. It's aptly subtitled 'the toughest footrace on Earth'. The race – as I quickly found out – is not for the faint-hearted. Temperatures amid the barren moonscapes of Morocco regularly touch 48°C, endless sand dunes make the simple act of running a tricky balancing act, and participants, as well as carrying all their own food and supplies, are obliged to camp communally in open-sided Berber tents.

By day six, most of the competitors, myself included, had been reduced to physical wrecks, badly blistered and half-starved. Stumbling across the sizzling Saharan plains in our scuffed footwear and unwashed clothes, we resembled a badly defeated retreating army, the heady exuberance of the starting line replaced by visions of our own mortality.

Yet, on the penultimate night, the race director, Patrick Bauer, announced that he had flown in musicians and a singer from the Paris Opera to perform a concert in our battered, Spartacus-like camp (in full evening dress no less). Rock'n'roll is normally my music of choice but, drunk with exhaustion, I'll never forget flopping down on my back under the star-speckled desert sky listening to the soothing strings and dulcet soprano and wondering why I hadn't really appreciated opera until that moment. It was one of the most bizarre, surreal and beautiful experiences of my travelling life, greatly enhanced by the exhausted, semi-hallucinogenic state I was in.

By Brendan Sainsbury

© Jean-Philippe Ksiazek | Getty

The Take Away

My best travel experiences tend to be spontaneous ones, but few have been as unexpected and memorable as this musical encounter in the middle of the desert, six days into a spirit-crushing endurance event. The music inspired me, picked me up and undoubtedly helped me stagger to the finish line the following day.

The Build Up

Despite its extreme nature, the Marathon des Sables is a popular race. It's best to start thinking about preparations at least two years in advance. Check out application details first on the official race website (marathondessables.com). Entry costs vary depending on your country of residence. From the UK, expect to pay in the vicinity of £4000, a fee that includes your race entry, flights, transfers, meals and post-race accommodation. The event normally takes place in late March and early April.

Training and physical preparation for the race shouldn't be taken lightly. The Marathon des Sables is not something you want to sign up for on a drunken bet. Above average fitness is a prerequisite even before you start your training programme. Furthermore, there's a long list of kit and equipment you'll need to purchase beforehand.

Ensure you visit your doctor for a full medical check-up before you send in your forms. You will be required to present a medical certificate to the race organisers prior to your application being accepted.

Lastly, if you want the pleasure without the pain, you can always attend the opera in Paris (operadeparis.fr).

Left: participants in the Marathon des Sables make the slog through the Sahara Desert
Above: exhausted competitors take some hard-earned R&R

52

FINDING PERSPECTIVE ON THE WEST COAST TRAIL

PACIFIC RIM NATIONAL PARK RESERVE, BC, CANADA

My husband and I stumbled out of our tent; the campsite was dark and everybody else was now sleeping. We had passed out earlier from the sheer exhaustion of the arduous day's hike through muddy pathways teeming with ancient roots, and along the ever-so-slippery sea shelf. Having not yet brushed our teeth, we headed towards the ocean, our toothbrushes in hand. As the waves gently lapped at the shore, the scent of campfire mingling with sea kelp punctuated the air. My husband turned off the flashlight and whispered, 'Look up...'

I was immediately dumbfounded. The sky was a truly black void, making the sparkling constellations and our Milky Way galaxy gleam brighter than I'd ever seen before. And the absolute clarity of the scene made me feel part of the greater picture – I was humbled by the universe.

We lay on our backs to absorb it all, and even caught glimpses of several shooting stars darting across the heavens. I may have still been caked in mud and covered in myriad scratches from my days on the West Coast Trail, but it didn't matter. Everything in my life had led me to this mesmerising moment, which I wished could last forever. This was where I was meant to be.

By Dayna Aamodt

The Take Away

That wondrous night left a huge imprint in my soul; I felt at peace with myself and regained a tremendous sense of childlike wonder of the world. And the 'big' problems that had occupied me before the hike were all put into perspective by the enormity and beauty of our universe.

The Build Up

The West Coast Trail, which weaves its way along 75km (47 miles) of coast in British Columbia's Pacific Rim National Park Reserve, is a breathtaking backcountry experience for advanced hikers. Each day, between 1 May and 30 September, just 75 overnight hikers are permitted on the trail.

Bookings are made in advance via Parks Canada (pc.gc.ca) – the reservation fee is $24.50 per person. Entry and exit points are at Pachena Bay, Gordon River and Nitinaht Lake. All overnight users of the trail must participate in a one-hour orientation session; pay the trail use fee ($127.50) and ferry crossing fee ($16); and register for a Trail Use Permit. There is an additional charge for a water taxi ($62.50) for hikers going between Nitinaht Village and Gordon River.

There are orientation sessions at Gordon River and Pachena Bay, daily at 10am and 2pm. Vehicles can be left at different locations near access points, and the West Coast Trail Express bus (trailbus.com) will return hikers to their starting points once the trail has been completed.

Left: *the night sky is just one of the many rewards of hiking the West Coast Trail*

53

DEATH AND REINCARNATION ON THE KORA

MT KAILASH, TIBET

I was stretched out full length, my head towards the holy mountain, at two of the four prostration points. Ahead soared the 5636m Drölma-la, a pass higher than Everest Base Camp and only a smidge lower than the summit of Kilimanjaro. Before I reached it I would need to die, symbolically at least, at Shiva-tsal. From there I was in the territory of the 'Lord of the Dead', and rebirth should follow at the top of the Drölma-la.

I was walking the kora, the three-day, 52km (32 mile) circuit of Mt Kailash, Tibet's holiest mountain. Having already passed the Bardo Trang sin test by squeezing my wider-than-expected hips underneath the legendary stone, I'd wipe clean my life's sin slate as long as I could struggle over the forbidding pass ahead. And if I wanted to wash away the sins of all my lifetimes? Well, that would require another 107 laps of the circuit. Tibetan Buddhism doesn't come easily.

First, however, tradition required that I leave something behind at Shiva-tsal, some reminder of the life I was leaving. A drop of blood or a lock of hair would do, but clearly many pilgrims opted for choice three, something they'd worn in their current lifetime. I found a stone carved with the Tibetan Buddhist chant Om Mani Padme Hum – 'Hail to the Jewel in the Lotus' – and respectfully draped my bright yellow spider-clad underpants below it.

By Tony Wheeler

The Take Away

Tibet is an amazing place, and walking the kora is an astounding journey on many levels – it taught me that moving on through life is important, and that I should always carry at least one item of clothing I don't mind leaving behind.

The Build Up

The trekking season for the kora runs from mid-May until mid-October, though snow can be encountered at high elevations at any time. Having your own tent and food is great for some, but accommodation and basic food is now available at Dira-puk and Zutul-puk. Teahouse tents encountered along the route sell water, noodles and – unsurprisingly – tea. If you have your own purifier, there are also plenty of natural water sources en route.

Most trekkers choose to carry their own gear or hire a local porter (¥210 per day), though horses and yaks are also available for hire in Darchen, the kora's small gateway town. Darche is a long and lonely 1200km (750 miles) from Lhasa, though the road has been much improved of late.

Independent travel is forbidden in Tibet, so organise your travel through a tour company. It should be able to organise the required Tibet Tourism Bureau (TTB) permit and the paperwork (an Aliens' Travel Permit; ATP) required for travel beyond Lhasa (up to 14 days is required to obtain the TTB permit). A hard-to-get Chinese visa is also required prior to departure.

Left: Mani stones, inscribed with Buddhist chants, can be found along the kora
Below: Tibet's holy Mt Kailash

54

JETTY OF JOY

ITELLEQ PIER, GREENLAND

It began, shamefully, with dishonesty. The sole passengers disembarking a small boat-bus at southern Greenland's wholly deserted Itelleq pier were myself and a Canadian lady who, while lovely, really liked to talk. And talk. Ahead of us, a beckoning trail sashayed up a grassy, sun-soaked hill en route to invisible Igaliku village, and the hotel where we were both to stay. The idea of having such an idyll soundtracked by perma-chatter was unthinkable – so, well, I fibbed. I dreamt up an urgent phone call that needed making. Leaving the motormouth to plod on a good distance ahead, I settled down at the short wooden jetty's end, phone fraudulently pressed to ear and legs happily dangling.

Slowly, it struck me: bar the pier and rough track, I couldn't see evidence of another soul. The loquacious lady was by now invisible round a fold of the knoll. Our boat had long passed off down the broad fjord. No planes flew overhead, and – common in sparsely populated Greenland – not a single building was evident. Best of all, there was just one sound: nearby, spearmint-coloured icebergs creaking and croaking. Nothing else. A complete, stunning serenity washed over me, followed by a profound and giddy calm. For the first time in years I had absolutely no sense of hurry, of worry; only the intense, joyous pleasure of being right in the moment. I felt sublimely happy, and more alive than ever before.

By Richard Mellor

The Take Away

Itilleq's pier has become a mental retreat for me at times of anxiety. When panic sets in, I imagine myself back on that empty jetty: my legs dangling, my breath slowing, and that blissful sense of calm and contentment. Back in the present, everything feels more manageable and put in perspective.

The Build Up

Boat-bus transfers from Qassiarsuk to Itilleq (aka Itivdleq) and accommodation at Igaliku Country Hotel can both be arranged through Blue Ice Explorer (blueice.gl), whose owner Jacky Simoud speaks good English. These activities usually form part of multi-centre itineraries following South Greenland's excellent trail network, in which one spends days hiking between farmstays and/or catered hotels. The region also supports cycling or horse-riding along the same routes, plus fishing, kayaking, whale-watching and much more. Visit Greenland's website

(greenland.com) lists trusted providers.

As there are virtually no bridges in South Greenland, road trips around the labyrinthine fjords are protracted. It's far quicker to hop aboard small ferry-style boats like the locals do, whizzing between icebergs. Blue Ice charters regular services, as does Disko Line (diskoline.dk). The 'How To Get Around' section on Visit Greenland's website is another good resource.

South Greenland's international airport, Narsarsuaq, has services to Copenhagen in Denmark with Air Greenland (airgreenland. com) and to much-nearer Reykjavik Airport – from where you can transfer by bus to Keflavik International Airport – with Air Iceland Connect (airicelandconnect.com). Both services run thrice-weekly, but only between early May and late September.

Above: icebergs off the coast of Greenland
Left: trawlers and other small vessels ferry tourists around the island's coastline

55

FORGETTING SOLITUDE IN THE GRAND CANYON

ARIZONA, USA

Trudging along the Bright Angel Trail in the chilly dawn, I spotted the graceful suspension bridge that spanned the Colorado River and linked this bank to the steep switchbacks up to the Grand Canyon's South Rim. I couldn't help but notice several women milling at its entrance. Was something wrong?

The group, I soon learned, were just catching their breath before the brutal ascent. As I prepared to start the climb, one turned and asked, 'What's your name?' A simple question, but one that encapsulated my trip.

I was in the canyon to ponder a life decision: stay in Los Angeles or move back east. Two days of strenuous solo hiking and hermit-style meditation would provide answers, I'd thought. But solitude was not to be.

My tiny hikers' dorm, where I'd slept the previous night after descending the South Kaibab Trail, was part of the famed Phantom Ranch. My 10-bunk cabin, one of two dorms for women, housed a lively crew: five dental hygienists on holiday from Canada, three stressed-out sisters on a birthday hike, and one woman who'd hiked the canyon carrying the adventure book A Short Walk in the Hindu Kush. Solo contemplation? Forget it. We shared snacks, Band-Aids, hiking tips and stories.

And the woman who asked my name the next morning? A bunker in the other women's dorm. She wasn't simply being friendly, rather the question was asked out of concern – to keep track of my whereabouts.

'Amy Balfour,' I replied then stepped onto the bridge. Energised anew.

By Amy C Balfour

Amy choosing the right path on her Grand Canyon trek

Above: sunrise over the Canyon, from Yavapai Point

No bones about it, Skeleton Point is just as awesome

The Take Away

The woman's concern, along with the stories and supplies shared with my bunkmates, highlighted what I'd been missing in LA – a sense that anyone had my back. Would the East Coast be any better? I didn't know, but this community of strangers helped pinpoint the problem and ultimately inspired me to move.

The Build Up

The South Kaibab Trail descends from the South Rim at Yaki Point to Phantom Ranch over some 11km (7 miles). Canyon views are vast and impressive along the way, but it's a steep trail with little shade and no water beyond the trailhead. Many hikers return on the 16km (10 mile) Bright Angel Trail, which includes a pleasant stop at shaded Indian Garden Campground.

For the best weather and hiking conditions, take this trip in spring or autumn. Summer temperatures in the canyon typically exceed 38°C. To maximise your time on the trail, catch the early-bird Hikers' Express Shuttle from the Bright Angel Lodge (shuttle times vary seasonally). Carry plenty of water.

Phantom Ranch, reached only by foot, mule ride or raft, offers cabins and single-sex dorms – it will be switching from a reservation system to an online lottery for stays beginning January 2019 (grandcanyonlodges.com). You can join the lottery 15 months in advance. Lucky solo hikers might be able to snag a bunk due to last-minute cancellations. Join the waiting list at the Bright Angel Lodge transportation desk the night before, then check back the next morning at the stated time.

TAKING THE PLUNGE WITH WHALE SHARKS

GULF OF TADJOURA, DJIBOUTI

With no land in sight and the knowledge that creatures from the deep were awaiting below, no one was more surprised than me when I leapt off a small rocking boat in the Gulf of Tadjoura. Terrified of the deep, and having never jumped off anything into water before, I plunged in with snorkel and mask in hand.

Spluttering to the surface, my thrill of not having sunk to the bottom was quickly overshadowed by the biggest dark mass passing several metres below my white legs. Its white spots moved slowly past like markings on a freight train, going on and on and on. This behemoth of a creature was but one of a family of whale sharks who were quite happily consumed by filter feeding on plankton in this random patch of sea. Seemingly surrounded by these gentle giants, I felt as if I had been dropped into a David Attenborough documentary on prehistoric fish.

And as I peacefully floated above them, like being suspended in the TV footage, my wonder was soon to overtake my fear. Despite just ducking beneath the water's surface, I felt as if I had peered into the past and met some ancient beings. Our oceans really are our last frontier.

By Georgina Wilson-Powell

The Take Away

Aside from the jubilation of getting over my fear of deep water (and the monsters of the past lurking in it), this experience also shaped my future. It awakened my consciousness of ocean issues, and much of my work today now deals with ways to get rid of marine plastics.

The Build Up

Djibouti, wedged between Eritrea, Ethiopia and Somaliland, sits at the entrance to the Red Sea from the Gulf of Aden. The country's capital, Djibouti City, is the main entry and exit point for the country – its Djibouti-Ambouli Airport welcomes a few dozen international flights each week. A new railway line also links the capital with Addis Ababa in Ethiopia.

The peak season for observing whale sharks is from November to January, when the silent beasts migrate here to mate and give birth in the Gulf of Tadjoura's warm waters, particularly in the Bay of Ghoubbet.

Dolphin (dolphinservices.com) is the only professional dive operator affiliated with CMAS and PADI that is based on the ground in the country – its equipment is well maintained, its facilities are well equipped and its staff are supremely knowledgeable, friendly and speak excellent English. Dolphin and Siyyan Travel & Leisure (dive-lucy. com), which is also accredited by PADI, offers live-aboard diving options for those wanting more time below the surface.

These responsible operators won't let you swim closer than 4m (13ft) to the whale sharks, so any dreams of touching one will need to be left at the water's edge (this is for your own wellbeing as well as that of the sharks).

Right: diving with whale sharks, the biggest fish on the planet

57

TOPPING EL TEIDE

TENERIFE, CANARY ISLANDS, SPAIN

It was 5am when I set out from the refuge, the beam of my headlight bouncing over the path ahead, volcanic pebbles crunching beneath my feet. The sea of clouds had dispersed overnight, revealing the great table of the Atlantic over 3000m below, glittering in starlight. Above, the roof of the volcano stood against the Milky Way, a shadow merging into space.

Drawn by a picture of El Teide's central snow-capped peak, I had come to the island of Tenerife two years prior to start a new kind of life. And from my hillside home I could see its great arc emerge from the sea and curve to its 3718m (12,198ft) summit, forming the tallest mountain in the Atlantic Ocean. The volcano was at once a daily symbol of hope, and also of reality, a constant reminder of the force of nature looming over my new life, a force capable of both beauty and destruction. But I had yet to experience the magic at the top, that legendary performance known locally as 'the Shadow'.

Reaching the summit just before sunrise, I looked out between two sulphurous pillars. And as the first rays lightened the sky, the great shadow of the mountain fell, rushing across the ocean to meet the distant curve of the planet. The long black triangle appeared like a celestial road, a road that stretched to the horizon. The world was truly full of wonders. Everything was going to be all right.

By Paul Stiles

Below: *the crater good: at the summit of Tenerife's volcanic El Teide*

© Michael Przech | 500px, © Paul Stiles

The shadow of El Teide, a stunning natural spectacle

The Take Away

We travel in search of wondrous moments. But why? They act like guides, revealing what is essential in life, while protecting us from the mundane, the trivial and the purely commercial. 'The Shadow' fell just at the right time, confirming that I was on the right path.

The Build Up

To see 'The Shadow' (a natural projection of the mountain itself), you must first ascend to El Refugio de Altavista, a mountain hut, and spend the night (€25). The easy way is to take the *teleférico* (cable car) from Teide National Park (9am-4pm, €13.50). Located on Hwy TF-21 at Km43, it has free parking and is accessible by bus from various points on the island. The *teleférico* ascends to 3555m, only 163m (535ft) below the summit. From here you descend to the refuge at 3270m (about an hour). The harder alternative is to hike up to the refuge from the *teleférico* parking lot (four to five hours). Plan to get there by 10pm.

The heated refuge is open year round, weather permitting, and holds 54 people. It comes with bedding, so sleeping bags are unnecessary. Drinks, water and limited cooking are available too. To reach the summit in time for sunrise requires a departure around 5am. Guests at the refuge do not need a permit to summit. As with most other things in nature, 'The Shadow' is weather dependent.

58

OCEANIC ODYSSEY

TRISTAN DA CUNHA,
SOUTH ATLANTIC OCEAN

I was 13 years old when I first saw it on a map. The island was so small that it was entirely obscured when I stuck in the pin to denote my plan to travel there some day. I didn't know anything more about it then, but over the years I learned that Tristan da Cunha was a British territory, home to 300 or so people and an active volcano. And when I discovered that it is the most remote inhabited island in the world, I knew I had to go.

Some 20 years after placing that pin, I found myself living in Cape Town. As I had done every few years, I looked into transport to the island, an airport-free speck in the South Atlantic Ocean, and realised I was in the best place on Earth for reaching it. Not being sure how long I'd be residing in the city meant one thing – there was to be no waiting around. I raided my honeymoon fund and my then-fiancé and I boarded a fishing boat.

Despite two decades of intermittent research, I'd failed to ever look into the sea conditions. Sadly I'm not a good sailor, and I was only an hour out of Cape Town when nausea struck. Three long days later I emerged from my cabin, almost fresh faced and still eager to arrive on Tristan.

Four days further on, the boat's engine ceased to hum. I climbed from my bunk and peered outside. There, perfectly framed in the porthole, was a distant Tristan. Feeling like a child on Christmas Eve, I slept fitfully, anticipating the moment I would finally set foot on the island I'd waited more than half my life to explore.

By Lucy Corne

Above: alone in the South Atlantic, Tristan da Cunha is the world's remotest inhabited island
Below: its capital is pleasingly called Edinburgh of the Seven Seas

The Take Away

Your teens are not easy years – nor most people's finest – but when I think back to that dream-fulfilling moment when I stepped onto Tristan, I salute my 13-year-old self and realise how crucial it is to never let go of those childhood dreams nor let anyone dissuade you from achieving them.

The Build Up

Fewer than a dozen boats leave Cape Town for Tristan each year, taking about six or seven days to make the crossing. Most are simple fishing boats that carry a few passengers and offer limited amenities, although hearty meals are included. Expect to pay around US$1000 for the return journey. The fanciest boat is the *SA Agulhas*, which leaves Cape Town once a year in September.

Accommodation on the island is in self-catering houses or homestays – both offer plenty of interaction with the islanders. There is a shop, a café and a pub, with crayfish, lamb and potatoes being the local specialities.

Activities on the island are simple ones: a hike up the volcano; a round of rustic golf, as chickens and cattle look on; tea and cake with some Tristan old-timers; or, if your stomach has recovered from the journey to get here, a boat trip to nearby Nightingale Island.

All trips need to be booked well in advance and permission to visit the island must be granted by the island council. All visitors to Tristan need to be flexible – you're at the whim of the elements and your trip could be extended for days or even weeks if the weather doesn't play along.

LOOKING UP TO THE WONDER OF ULURU

ULURU-KATA TJUTA NATIONAL PARK, AUSTRALIA

I was only nine, but the significance of Uluru wasn't lost on me. I was standing at the spiritual heart of Australia and every breath felt sacred. Even from a distance it commanded attention. As we trundled down the red road, our kombi stirring flocks of black galahs out of dusty canopies, each of us shrieked with excitement as we caught our first glimpses of the famous monolith through the scrub. An orange mass glowing against the brilliant blue sky, the sight was familiar but surreal, as though it were painted on the horizon.

Up close, I was intimidated by Uluru's size and rough exterior. While my brother scrambled gleefully up the rock face, I hesitated. The leap from 'chicken rock' near the base to the chain handrail a little further up was too much for my racing heart. I slipped back down, hot tears stinging my eyes, and took the path less travelled with my mum instead.

I'm still glad I did. The traditional custodians request that visitors don't climb Uluru, and it became crystal clear to me why as we wandered slowly, reverently around its base. Here was a cathedral chiselled from countless wet season downpours; there were the records of ancient songlines hand painted on the sandstone. Each step of the track revealed a little more of Uluru's secrets, its unfathomable history and its mysterious ancestral guardians. This was no rock to be conquered, but a place of worship.

By Penny Carroll

The Take Away

Absorbing the magic of Uluru at such a young age undoubtedly shaped me – it woke my imagination and deepened my connection to the Australian landscape, but most of all it left me with an unshakeable belief in a force at work in the universe greater than any of us.

The Build Up

Uluru (formerly known as Ayers Rock) stands 450km (280 miles) from Alice Springs in Australia's Red Centre. You can fly direct to Ayers Rock Airport, or take a four-and-a-half hour road trip from Alice Springs. If you're driving and have a few days to spare, the Red Centre Way winds past other impressive outback sights such as Kings Canyon and the West MacDonnell ranges.

Time your trip carefully to make the most of your Uluru pilgrimage. Between May and September you can expect clear, crisp days that make exploring the rock more comfortable; in summer, the scorching heat will mean you'll need to plan your walk around Uluru before 11am, and the park will close if weather conditions look dangerous. A three-day visitor pass to the national park is $25 and can be purchased at the entry station on your way into Uluru.

Climbing Uluru is considered culturally insensitive, and as of October 2019 it will be banned. Instead, take the 10.6km (6½ mile) loop walk around the base to see the rock up close, or head to a viewing platform at dawn or dusk to watch in awe as Uluru's colours transform before your eyes.

Left: *although climbing Uluru will be banned in 2019, it's always been best to view it by walking around the base*

60

EMERGING FROM THE GOBI DESERT

MONGOLIA

A thousand miles of nothingness was now behind us, and I stood for a moment with my two companions contemplating the safety that lay just a few miles ahead. For six weeks, no one in the outside world had known our exact whereabouts. We had walked 30 miles a day on average, side-stepping snakes and navigating landscapes of rock, red sand and gravel. Sometimes we had chanced upon nomads and they had guided us to their wells. Usually, though, we were just walking, alone and in total silence, as if we were traversing a strange and often hostile planet, and all the time the huge blue skies of Mongolia bearing down.

My two companions were not humans but camels – and not always very reliable ones, at that. In more arduous stretches they had tried to prise open my drink containers. However, a third camel, Jigjik, had walked off home and the fact that the others (Bert, who had only one eye, and a massive creature called Bastion, who was loath to carry anything much) had stuck by me meant an enormous amount – not just because they carried my supplies and I'd be dead without them.

Unlike other domesticated animals, camels do not need humans. They have a perfect array of adaptations – the fatty humps, the wide

feet, the prehensile lips for stripping bushes. Yet these two camels had accepted me as 'top camel', that I would lead them and care for them – perhaps they distrusted the wolves that we sometimes heard howling at night. And in turn I was grateful for their co-operation; lately I had even taken to sharing my muesli, though it wasn't so very different from the grass out here.

But now it was over. Day after day I'd heard only the wind, the squeak of leather harnesses and the jangling of the baggage, but now the journey across the Gobi was done. And in the

Benedict and one of his indispensable travel companions

Above: the Gobi's desolate desert landscape

The region's terrain is arid and inhospitable

nick of time! Back in September, when I'd set out, the sheer heat of the wind had blistered my lips but now winter was fast approaching. Snowflakes drifted by; the water that we carried was often frozen solid.

Yet suddenly I found myself reluctant to take another step towards the outside world – the world where I belonged. I had made it; I was safe and sound; perhaps today I'd be able to make a call home. However, standing there on the desert edge, the first sign of humanity was the litter now being carried on the breeze. I watched a pink bag as it came tumbling towards me, snagging briefly in the scrub, while somewhere far off came the rumble of a goods truck.

At that moment, as I prepared to re-join my own kind, I realised the extent to which I'd adapted to the beautiful and starkly terrifying Gobi. I knew then how much I would miss it – and the camel companions too. Together we had made passage through a thousand miles of pristine oblivion and out the other side.

By Benedict Allen

The Take Away

Probably no one had ever travelled right across the Gobi alone on foot before – but that's beside the point. This wasn't about planting a flag or achieving a 'first', it was about coming to terms with a place that had once seemed so alien and threatening but which I'd now made home.

The Build Up

The Gobi Desert is a vast arid area straddling the border between Mongolia and China. Travelling here is best done in the spring or autumn to avoid the heat of summer (when it can be as high as 40ºC) and cold of the winter (when the temperature plunges to -40ºC). If you're planning on following in the footsteps of this journey, autumn is best as the camels will have had the spring and summer to gain much-needed weight. In order to maintain control of your humped companions, you really need to lead them on foot. Three camels is ideal for such an expedition, with two carrying supplies each day and one in turn having a day off. This adventure travelled eastwards from Ej Uul towards Zamyn-Üüd on the border with China. The journey of six weeks covers some 2000km (1250 miles).

If you'd rather just get a taste of the region, there are plenty of shared minivans, taxis, jeeps and public buses to the Gobi province capitals from Ulaanbaatar. Flights are also an option from the capital to Dalanzadgad and Altai. From China, it's possible to reach the border and cross at Zamyn-Üüd and then continue on to Gobi towns such as Sainshand. Organising tours of the Gobi is best done in Ulaanbaatar.

Right: *desert dunes are a feature of southern Mongolia*
Below: *the area's only credible means of transportation*

SPERM WHALES GATHERING

ATLANTIC OCEAN

I was alone in the middle of the Atlantic Ocean, months into my voyage, and found myself mystified. The sounds of nearby dolphins would radiate through the hull of my rowing boat, resembling an excitable transistor radio whirring and whistling for reception. But this was different. Deeper and louder, it was clicking and tapping.

I rolled over in the tiny cabin and put my ear to my water bottles, which occasionally made odd noises in the heat. No wiser, I started checking my electronics and batteries. After 20 minutes of fruitless efforts I decided to check out on deck.

As I stepped up I was greeted with the answer – a pod of four sperm whales swimming (and singing) just 10 metres (33ft) away. Dwarfing my 7m-long boat were two large females, and joining them were a couple of calves about half the size. They were rolling at the surface, almost appearing to be yawning, and I could see their tiny lower jaws and rows of pegged teeth protruding oddly from their massive, blocky heads. Intriguingly, scars down their flanks told stories of hunting giant squid a thousand metres below the surface.

To get a better look at me they started spy-hopping – standing upright in the water, exposing their eyes and enormous heads. They also upturned, sticking their huge tail flukes into the air. All the while I was transfixed, staring and grinning as I took in every minute detail. Although this sublime encounter was incredibly charged, it was deeply peaceful too.

By Sarah Outen

The Take Away

Looking in the whales' eyes, I felt a beautiful connection, but also a sense of guilt for humanity's damage to their oceans. (I saw more plastic than whales during my 150-day voyage between Cape Cod and the UK.) I have committed to publicise the problem and to consume more consciously.

The Build Up

Ocean rowing is not really about the rowing – it's more about looking after yourself at sea, making good decisions and being adaptable, resilient and self-reliant. Many of these attributes are actually needed just to get to the start line; preparation is generally an exhausting and expensive project, with many people not making it. Don't just focus on physical training, as mental preparation is key – it's often the latter that will get you through when at sea.

Food is really important as both fuel and morale booster; packing simple-to-prepare, nutritious and lightweight meals, with a variety of textures and flavours, is a recipe for success.

Weather is always a wild card, but heading out with full respect for it, and an attitude of acceptance towards whatever it throws at you, is a good position to aim for. Day-to-day life at sea can be monotonous and gruelling, but equally beautiful and rewarding, so it's important to try to live in the moment. And remember... every storm will pass.

Left: Just who is looking at whom? Sharing glances with sperm whales in the mid-Atlantic

62

A WINDOW INTO ANTARCTICA

DECEPTION ISLAND, ANTARCTICA

From a god's-eye view, it looks a little like Pac-Man's skull – almost a complete circle, but not quite. The cataclysm that ruptured the side of Deception Island, allowing the ocean to flood its caldera to form a perfect bay, may have taken place over 10,000 years ago, but the crater remains that of an active volcano.

Before we set foot ashore for our final landing, the expedition's staff told us that this thermal activity keeps the water by the shore warmer. As was the case with most of our shore landings in Antarctica, time was essentially our own – we could swim in this allegedly warm water if we wanted to, as long as we didn't miss the last transfer back to the ship.

Instead of choosing to spend some time down on the smouldering beach with bemused chinstrap penguins, I decided to instead embark on the stiff climb up to The Window, a small crack in Deception's volcanic crown.

The ground underfoot wasn't easy to navigate, being a mixture of melting snow and biscuity, black rock. Progress felt slow and I was very much aware of my time constraints. Soon enough, though, the sound of the penguins on the shore died away, even if the faint reek of their guano did not.

Hot and breathless, I arrived at The Window. Through one side, I could see Neptune's

Bellows, the dramatic entrance into the haphazard bay, while behind me the Polar Pioneer rested at anchor. In that moment, I wasn't just looking back at the ship but on the entire Antarctic expedition, which was the most thrilling trip of my life.

By Jamie Lafferty

The Take Away

Was Deception the singularly most beautiful place I visited in Antarctica? Probably not. But it was my final look at the world's most pristine place. On that last landing, it felt as though all the memories and beauty of the trip were waiting for me at the top of the volcano.

The Take Away

Deception Island is one of the traditional final stops before ships make the tumultuous two-day crossing back across the Drake Passage to South America. Whereas Whalers Bay provides shelter and the opportunity to enjoy and endure a 'polar plunge', the island's outer shore is home to a mega colony of tens of thousands of chinstrap penguins.

Visiting the island at all is a matter of chance. Although many smaller Antarctic expeditions plan to stop there, a combination of timings and inclement weather may render it impossible. Even so, the *Polar Pioneer*, which sails to the seventh continent from November to April, normally aims to have Deception as its final Antarctic destination. Due to a capacity of just 56 passengers, the converted Russian ship from the Cold War era is able to make the most of its three-hour landing slot at Deception.

Most companies that operate voyages in the region offer a wide array of itineraries, with prices varying depending on duration, cabin and optional activities, including snorkelling and diving, as well as kayaking.

Above: Deception Island in Antarctica, the caldera of an active volcano
Left: chinstrap penguins gather in large numbers on the island

A WRITER'S VISION

NONG KHAI TO BANGKOK, THAILAND

It's what some people call a 'gap year', but to me it was less a gap than a change in direction. Worn down by the confrontation and the mean-spiritedness of the public debate in Australia, I left my career as a lawyer working with asylum seekers and took off on a one-way ticket to see the world. Perhaps I was looking for inspiration. Though more likely, I wasn't quite sure where I was heading.

My journey began in Bangkok and shifted north to the Mekong River. For three days I drifted downriver in a cargo boat, shopping in local markets, sleeping in village huts by the riverbank and soaking up the pristine silence of riverine forests. By Vientiane, however, I was restless and ready to move on. I crossed into Thailand to Nong Khai and boarded an early morning train that was bound for Bangkok.

I travelled third class, and for long hours I found myself sitting in the open doorway of the carriage watching the picturesque simplicity of rural Thai life speed past.

And then it happened. Without warning, I knew with sudden clarity that I wanted to be a writer. So powerful was the sensation, so unexpected was the emotional earthquake that I cast an involuntary glance skywards, half-expecting a ray of sunlight to pierce the clouds. There was euphoria in that moment, a true sense of calling, the intensity that comes from finding the answer to longings that were, until that moment, only half understood. My new life had begun.

By Anthony Ham

The Take Away

That moment changed the direction of my life forever. Although it would take a year to begin making my living in this way, it was the day that launched my career as a writer. The clarity of that day's vision has never wavered in the two decades since.

The Build Up

Thailand's rail system has modernised since the days when it was possible to sit with your legs hanging out the open door of the carriage and watch the world go by – it may be possible on some local trains but speedier long-haul services are more security conscious these days. But some things haven't changed – the impossibly green rice fields, the improbable hills rising in strange shapes from the plains, the friendliness of the Thai people with whom you'll share the train.

There are four daily services from Nong Khai to Bangkok, but three of these deposit you in the Thai capital in the wee small hours of the morning and travel the entire route in darkness. Train No 76, the only service that enables you to enjoy the passing scenery by travelling the 621km (386 miles) through the daylight hours, departs from Nong Khai at 7am and arrives in Bangkok 10 hours later at 5.10pm. Fares start at 497B for first class, 238B for second and 103B for third; in the latter class you may not have a seat, but hanging out the window and maybe even the door is far more likely to be part of the experience.

Left: a Buddhist monk walks a station platform in Thailand

IT'S NOT ABOUT THE BUCKET LIST

CAÑÓN DEL COLCA, PERU

After a three-hour bus ride from Arequipa, my wife and I looked at our guidebook for the next move to reach Cañón del Colca, the world's second-deepest canyon. We scanned the text, looked at the road sign, then back at the book. We were in the wrong town and the next bus didn't leave until the following day. Although infuriated with ourselves, we were still determined to get there.

Things took a turn for the better when a cabbie offered to take us to a nearby lookout. So off we went into the depths of the Andes, hugging the mountain curves, each etched with rice terraces and speckled with thatched houses. Rounding a corner we were then stopped in our tracks by a fiesta of elderly Peruvians in the middle of the road. We crept forwards, assuming they'd move aside, but instead a woman in traditional embroidered dress knocked on our window. 'Come dance!' she said in Spanish with a smile. 'You may not pass, until you dance!'

My wife and I looked at each other, and then simultaneously swung open our doors. The partygoers cheered and the wooden instruments grew louder. We were pulled into a circle of twirling ladies, and around and around we went, with leg kicks and hip shakes. Soon we were partaking in overflowing shots of heady chicha (corn brew). We continued to dance, arm in arm with our new amigas, until dark. We happily never made it to Cañón del Colca.

By Mike Howard

The Take Away

Like so many others, we were focused on ticking off our bucket list. It took a band of dancing Peruvians to remind us to slow down, embrace the detours and relish in wherever we are. We also learned that it's the people that make each place so special.

The Build Up

Although twice as deep as the Grand Canyon, the 3270m (10,700ft) abyss that is the Cañón del Colca is fascinating for more than its scale alone – it's a destination rich in natural beauty, hikes, culture, history and tradition. This street dancing extravaganza was due to the visit coinciding with the Fiesta de Las Cruces, celebrated in many Peruvian highland regions on 3 May.

Most people access the Cañón del Colca region from Chivay, which is a 3½-hour bus journey from Arequipa. From Chivay's Terminal Terrestre you can then catch another bus to reach Cruz del Condor (90 minutes), where condors nest and effortlessly soar in the updraft. A taxi can get you to this lookout in half that time and offers you the chance of unforgettable pit-stops at traditional villages and dramatic vistas. For a multi-day stay, base yourself in the charming town of Cabanaconde.

All visitors to the region are required to get a *boleto turistico* (S70) for entrance into the key sites. These are available at a booth just outside Chivay on the road from Arequipa.

Left: our author, his wife and new friends in Peru
Below: Peru's great Cañón del Colca is one of the deepest in the world

65

SNOWED-OUT ON WUTAI SHAN

SHANXI PROVINCE, CHINA

Through the day the snow had built afresh, layer upon layer. The night before I had stepped from a bus into a whiteout on the Buddhist mountain of Wutai Shan in Shanxi province, glowing Chinese faces pressed against steamed-up windows as the blizzard swallowed me whole. My hands had finally found a temple spirit wall, and I swept snowflakes from the carved Chinese characters – 殊像寺 (Shuxiang Si, meaning 'Shuxiang Temple') – that announced my monastic lodgings for the night.

The next morning, the hefty temple doors creaked open to a mountain panorama of the purest, softest white beneath a cold, sapphire sky. The mountain temple community was almost bereft of visitors: no buses in, no buses out. We were sealed off by snow. I encountered a huge, placid dog sitting motionless by a temple stupa, entranced even, watching the mountains. I stayed with him a long time, and by then the first new snow had begun to fall. Wandering through temple grounds, I had seen it thicken again, large flakes the size of duck down.

A premature twilight soon darkened Wutai Shan as the wind picked up, filling the sky with sound, which then became a roar. I found myself alone, between somewhere and my temple home, at the heart of this storm that mixed snow with a shrieking, funnelling vortex of noise beyond which I could hear trees crashing down on the mountainside. I can't remember how long I stood there, just listening and listening, and feeling I could listen to that sound for ever.

By Damian Harper

Damian wasn't the only one entranced by the snow

A temple stupa fades into the blizzard

The Take Away

My travel plans had been thrown into disarray by events beyond my control, but this was a blessing in disguise. Though my itinerary had gone out of the window, staying put to experience my situation to the full taught me that even seasoned travellers can be totally poleaxed by unforeseen events and upended by what they accidentally discover.

The Build Up

The mountains of Wutai Shan, located at altitude in northern China, are not too hard to reach but require a bit of planning. The winter months there are largely too cold, with an abundance of snow and ice. The events described here occurred in late April/early May, so late spring to late summer are more ideal times to visit. Take warm, waterproof clothing and hiking boots, whatever the season (the temperature can drop considerably at night). It's a vast area, so to fully enjoy it, give yourself three or more days.

Most people reach Wutai Shan by bus from Beijing, Datong or Taiyuan; Wutai Shan train station is actually at Shahe, 50km (31 miles) away and connected to Wutai Shan by bus. The admission fee to Wutai Shan is rather steep at ¥218, which includes a mandatory ¥50 transport charge (valid for three days in the region). Some of the temples charge an additional entrance fee, including the remote Nanchan Temple and Foguang Temple, home to some of the oldest surviving wooden buildings in China. Accommodation is not too hard to find and there are several restaurants, but the choice is limited.

Above: *Tibetan prayer flags fly over the town of Taihuai in Wutai Shan*

SOUL FOOD ON MT BIERSTADT

COLORADO, USA

After a particularly rough summer in which I lost my best friend to leukaemia, I took some time off and travelled with my brother to Colorado to clear my head. I have a general love of mountains and a tendency towards crazy schemes, so I got the wild idea that we should hike one of Colorado's infamous 'fourteeners' (peaks over the elevation of 14,000ft/4267m). Both of us were in decent shape, but neither of us had done any training for a hike of that magnitude.

My brother is typically keen to go along with most of my harebrained ideas, and this case was no different. The next morning, we set out into the Rockies at 4am to begin our ascent of 4287m (14,065ft) Mt Bierstadt, which Google had assured me was the easiest of the bunch. Clearly, 'easy' is a relative term – we started wheezing quickly and spent hours dragging ourselves up the mountain, having to stop continuously to catch our breath in the thinning air.

The effort felt appropriate to the emotional turmoil I had been feeling all summer, and with each step upwards, I fought a little harder to find within myself the will to keep going. When we finally reached the top, eye level with the clouds, we were greeted with the most spectacular view, which was made so much more perfect by how hard it had been to earn it.

By Laura Brown

The Take Away

Standing on the summit, I could feel the sadness that had been shrouding my soul all summer start to melt away, revealing a new version of myself. I've never felt more powerful or free than I did at that moment, and never had as good a night's sleep as I did after we climbed down.

The Build Up

The US state of Colorado has 53 fourteeners, which range in elevation from 14,007ft/4269m (Sunshine Peak) to 14,440ft/4401m (Mt Elbert). At 14,065ft (4287m), Mt Bierstadt ranks 38th on the illustrious list. As you'd expect, the levels of difficulty to climb vary widely depending on the length, gradient and condition of the respective trails. The return hike to the top of Mt Bierstadt from the trail head at Guanella Pass is just over 11km and rises over 865m.

Guanella Pass sits on the aptly named Guanella Pass Scenic Byway, which provides incredible views of the Rockies, particularly Mt Evans and Mt Bierstadt. Along the route that links the town of Grant (on US 285) to the south and Georgetown (on Interstate 70) to the north, you'll likely catch a view of a bighorn sheep or three.

Incredibly, in 2015, 40-year-old Denver native Andrew Hamilton summited all the fourteeners in nine days, 21 hours and 51 minutes.

Left: *the sign says it all on Mt Bierstadt, the 38th highest of Colorado's fourteeners*

67

TOUCHING TIBET

ARUNACHAL PRADESH, INDIA

Fired by a desire to reach the longhouse before nightfall, we walked fast, our feet drumming rhythmically on the ground as we went. Ajidu, my Idu guide, strode ahead; descending nimbly into elfish dells, weaving through lush pockets of jungle and sliding across slabs of rock at the bottom of small, gabbling waterfalls. And every time we emerged into the open there was the white wall of Tibet, ranged like a snowy sentinel across the northern horizon.

That afternoon I felt my whole being fill with light and happiness, as if every joyous stride was sloughing off the last remnants of an unwanted skin. It wasn't just the exhilaration of walking through this unknown wilderness: it was that I realised, in those few hours, that the awful months of panic attacks I'd experienced in the past year were just that, the past. It was one of those rare occasions in life when you feel a pure, unrestrained joy to be alive, right here, right now.

At dusk we reached a single bamboo longhouse on a knoll above the river. The last dwelling before Tibet, its inhabitants were an elderly Idu Mishmi couple who'd never clapped eyes on a foreigner before. We spent the night drinking homemade rice wine around their fire, all of us equally fascinated by the foreign alien in front of them, the hut filled with the noise of our increasingly drunken laughter. I can't remember having spent a happier day in my entire life.

By Antonia Bolingbroke-Kent

Antonia's generous hosts, and pets, outside their longhouse

Our writer makes her bed for the night ↙

The Take Away

Walking through these remote hills was a wonderful experience in itself. But what made it extraordinary was the sudden realisation that I was healed, that my panic attacks were indeed behind me. It felt like emerging euphorically into the light after a lengthy spell in darkness.

The Build Up

The Indian state of Arunachal Pradesh is the most north-easterly point of the subcontinent; a little-known Himalayan state that lies folded between the Tibetan Plateau, Burma, Bhutan, Nagaland and Assam's Brahmaputra Valley. A disputed border region, it's claimed by China as South Tibet and was only opened to tourism in the late 1990s. Today it remains a restricted area and anyone wishing to travel there must apply for an Inner Line Permit from the Indian government. Permits are only issued to groups of two or more and allow you to travel in specified areas for up to 30 days. The cost depends on how many are in your group, how you apply (directly or through a local travel agent), where you want to go and how long you wish to be there. With a great deal of wrangling, however, it is possible to get permission to travel solo across the state (as Antonia did for two months), though when near the border a local guide is mandatory.

The best time to trek is between October and November.

Above: *villages dot the verdant mountainsides of Arunachal Pradesh*

A STRING OF BLACK PEARLS

ICELAND

The massive stone sea arch at Dyrhólaey

William Morris rode around Iceland on a horse in 1871. I went there driving a 4WD in 2017. It's an elemental place, and driving the south coast did not lead to one moment so much as a series of them, strung out along the coastline over several twilights. A string of black pearls.

In painting classes I'm taught to make background colours recessive, cooler, to suggest perspective. Such rules don't hold sway here, where the sky that roils, throbs, is alive with a light. The landscape feels sentient. It makes perfect sense that stories of elves and fairies, of álagablettir (places of enchantment) have such a hold here. As I drive I feel disorientated by the physiological effect of the compressed light, a stormy darkness competing with the endless day.

On my first night I stand on a black beach, under a black and stormy sky, in the strange glow of midnight. The light does something to my brain, as if I'm on the inside of a dream. I stand there for an hour or so, staring at the horizon. On my second night I look into a tunnel of grey cloud settled over a glacier. Background looms into foreground, a volcano lifts into the clouds, and the flash of ice blue in the centre of that strange glowing-green light looks like an eye. On a third, as I drive towards the glacier lagoon, a gust of wind gets under my car, lifts it up slightly, then places me gently back on the road.

By Sophie Cunningham

Seasonal blizzards envelop an Icelandic church

The Take Away

This light – neither day, nor night – creates a space where conscious and unconscious blur. It's a powerful space. I understand that our plundered planet could, if it chose, toss us humans off with not much more than a shrug. I don't feel fear, so much as awe.

The Build Up

Southwestern Iceland, perhaps the country's most enchanting corner, is known for many things – plummeting waterfalls, geothermal geysers, gleaming icecaps, ominous volcanoes – but it's the black volcanic beaches that tend to inspire the most captivation.

Some sublime stretches are found in the vicinity of island's most southerly village, Vík, which sits 180km (112 miles) southeast of Reykjavík along the Ring Road (Rte 1). A short drive west out of town leads to Rte 215, which branches off to the south – follow it for 5km (3 miles) along the base of the Reynisfjall ridge to Reynisfjara, a magical black beach backed by stacks of basalt columns that resemble a church organ. It also offers exceptional views of the huge stone sea arch at Dyrhólaey, one of the south coast's most famous natural formations. The latter is reached a little further west along the Ring Road, via Rte 218. Its black beaches are also remarkable, as are the views from atop the promontory.

For moody skies, incredible light and moments of solitude, visit Iceland's south coast during the shoulder seasons of May and September – it's also more affordable than in high season.

Below: a sandstorm darkens the sky over a volcanic beach near Vík with an ominous black cloud

69

FLYING FLIP-FLOPS AND THE BIRKENSTOCK

HANOI, VIETNAM

With a whopping clank the Coke can flew skywards and into the darkness of the night. The crowds erupted and I ran gleefully, arms raised and one foot bare, to retrieve my weapon of mass destruction – a size 46 Birkenstock sandal.

An hour earlier, as I wandered the damp streets of Hanoi's Old Quarter, I stopped to watch an intriguing street game being played by kids. It involved flip-flops being hurled at the said can. Soon the rules became apparent: miss, and you walk to retrieve your sandal in disgrace, then stand 'trapped' behind the can (and its keeper); strike it, and you run wildly to get your footwear before the keeper can tag you with the can. Successful throws also free 'trapped' participants and shower you with adulation.

With a mix of excited and sceptical looks (from the children and their parents, respectively), I was encouraged to try. Eyes bulged and jaws dropped – clearly nobody had ever seen what an ultimate-playing Vancouverite could do with a Birkenstock. As word of my prowess spread, crowds grew on the pavement. Every time I stepped up, they all started chanting loudly. I don't know what it translated to, perhaps: 'He's big. He's crazy. He sure can throw!' And after each triumphant can battering a little boy would tug at my shirt sleeve, his face beaming, his thumb raised.

How did my right foot feel after running barefoot across the hard pavement for an entire evening? Great – it never touched the ground.

By Thomas Mills

© Matt Munro, © Tran Anh Linh | 500px

The Take Away

I guess I knew that laughter and sport were both
international languages, but until that evening I
never realised just how powerful they could be.
Engaging with cultures and sharing moments of
commonality are among life's greatest rewards.

The Build Up

It's not hard to find fun and games in the Old Quarter
of Vietnam's capital city, whether it's kids running
riot with flip-flops in the tangled streets, hipsters
playing Chinese chess on pavements or wizened
octogenarians practising t'ai chi by Hoan Kiem
Lake. An initiative launched in 2016 to close some
of the streets around the lake to vehicle traffic on
weekends and holidays, has led to a profusion of other
traditional games being played there – try your hand
at bamboo jacks, stilt walking, skipping, tug of war
and Mandarin square capturing, to name but a few.

Negotiating the Old Quarter's streets when they are
in full flood, however, can be an intimidating experience
at first – constant streams of motorcycles whiz and
beep between jams of cars and make crossing the
street a challenging sport in itself. Spend a little time
wandering them though, and you'll start to absorb
the frenetic spirit of this gritty neighbourhood, a place
where commerce has raged for over a thousand years.

Left: vendors and all manner of vehicles share
Hanoi's lively streets
Above: the Vietnamese capital illuminated at dusk

70

WILD CAMPING IN WALES

SNOWDONIA NATIONAL PARK, WALES

Phoebe finds her single-person Snowdonia pitch

Footsteps. Quiet, but definite, were headed my way. Despite being cocooned in the warmth of my sleeping bag, I felt my entire body go cold. Before I'd come on this, my first solo wild camp, I'd laughed at those who'd told me that I might be attacked, mugged or eaten by a bear (there are no bears in Wales). But as I lay there in the shadow of the Nantlle Ridge's rocky spine, vulnerable and alone, my cockiness was gone.

Not that things hadn't already gone a little wrong. I'd been chastised by a youth group for being uncool (they were there by coercion – I was there by choice), eaten alive by midges, chased by sheep, and sunburnt by the unpredictably good Welsh weather. Yet doing this by myself was so important.

I steadied myself, opened the zip of my tent door and peered out into the darkness, calling: 'Is someone there?' Soon my head torch revealed the true identity of my attacker... a rabbit. I couldn't help but laugh at myself. Of course there is no one lurking in the wilderness in wait for wild campers. I slept soundly after that.

Back at my car the following afternoon I caught sight of myself in the rearview mirror – my hair plastered to my face, which was red from the sun and puckered with midge bites – and though I'd never looked so unglamorous, I'd never felt so good.

By Phoebe Smith

© Justin Foulkes. © Phoebe Smith

Preparing for an alfresco meal with her gas stove

The Take Away

I had done it – set myself a challenge that scared me and survived, relying on no one else. From then on I knew three things: I was a wild camping addict, I could do anything I put my mind to, and life would never be the same again.

The Build Up

Wild camping is essentially sleeping out away from a proper campsite. You don't get the comfort of a toilet block or showers, but then you also don't get noisy neighbours (apart from the occasional rabbit), the confines of designated pitches or charged for the pleasure.

Although in many places around the world wild camping is legal and encouraged (particularly in Scandinavia), in the UK it's only legal in Scotland (though restrictive new bylaws in Loch Lomond and The Trossachs National Park make some lakeshores exempt from this) and Dartmoor National Park in England. Elsewhere you are supposed to ask for the landowner's permission. This is often wildly impractical and often impossible so it is typically tolerated if you stick to the wild campers' code: be discreet, arrive late and leave early, leave no trace of your camp, bury toilet waste at least 30m (100ft) from any water source, avoid lighting a fire, stay away from paths and people's houses, and move on if asked to do so.

Required kit includes a tent or bivvy bag, a good sleeping mat and bag, a head torch, stove (and gas) for purifying water, water bottle, lots of food and warm layers.

Below: Snowdonia National Park in North Wales

TRACKING DESERT ELEPHANTS

KUNENE REGION, NAMIBIA

Along the sun-scorched Hoanib Riverbed, deep within the barren Namib Desert, just 80km from the isolated Skeleton Coast, our 4WD crept along in first gear. With the engine humming gently, my guide and I perched beady-eyed on the edge of our clammy leather seats, desperate to catch a glimpse of one of Africa's rarest and largest animals. Despite the fading light of dusk, the temperature still hovered at a sweltering 42°C.

We had enough food and water to last 24 hours, but just 30 minutes from our previous night's camp, with our tyres edging quietly through the cocoa-coloured mud, a family of vast Namib Desert elephants emerged from the glistening mirage in the middle distance. There are believed to be just 100 or so desert elephants in an area of almost 120,000 sq km, and we'd stumbled across six of them.

With a lolloping calf at its centre, the herd stripped dusty foliage from the parched riverbank. As their grey, crusty skin took on an auburn tinge in the softening sunlight, I sipped a frosty bottle of lager, transfixed by the elephants' gigantic majesty. I was overcome with an immense feeling of privilege, but also embarrassment. The whole encounter had unfolded so quickly and unexpectedly. Hundreds of kilometres from human civilisation, we had been granted a candid perspective on one of the planet's most endangered species.

By Simon Parker

The Take Away

As a journalist I often rely upon beginnings, middles and ends to tell my stories. However, this experience taught me that the animal kingdom has no such respect for these very human narrative conventions. We were prepared to search for many hours, but they appeared when we least expected them.

The Build Up

Tracking desert elephants is typically a drawn-out affair, and as their name would suggest, their habitat is hot, isolated and rather difficult to explore without the assistance of an experienced local guide and a 4WD. There are also just two places on the planet to spot them: Namibia and Mali, and their numbers are in sharp decline.

The Kunene Region in northwest Namibia is, however, where you're most likely to find these elephants. There are a handful of desert camps in the region that provide tracking experiences, but be warned, these are rarely cheap and can often only be reached by small plane.

Thrifty travellers could opt to hire a freelance local guide – make sure they're well stocked with food and water, should you become stranded. Be aware that mobile phones don't work in the area and there are prides of desert lions who regularly stalk their prey along the Hoanib River.

Left: the landscape of he remote Kunene Region, where rare desert elephants can sometimes be found

72

WATCHING LAVA FLOW

GALÁPAGOS ISLANDS, ECUADOR

I was living a lifelong dream by touring the Galápagos Islands by boat. We'd already spent several days touring around the western part of the archipelago, having some of the most amazing wildlife encounters I've ever experienced: watching blue-footed boobies and marine iguanas; snorkelling with manta rays and sea turtles; and observing the islands' giant tortoises.

It was midway through the trip and we were anchored off Isabela, one of the largest islands of the group. In the middle of the night, when everyone was fast asleep in their cabins, the intercom suddenly crackled into life and the captain asked us all to come up on deck. Bleary-eyed, we pulled on our coats, stumbled out of our cabins and made our way to the top deck. Kiké, the ship's naturalist, was waiting for us there, a huge grin on his face. He pointed to the horizon, and said, 'Look. Wolf Volcano is erupting.'

Sure enough, on the skyline, one of Isabela's craggy black peaks was spewing out a huge pillar of smoke and ash. Its summit glowed white and red rivers of lava were streaming down its slopes. As we got closer, we could even smell sulphur in the air and see the

columns of steam billowing skywards as the lava hit the sea. It felt like we were watching the beginning of life on Earth.

By Oliver Berry

Blue-footed
boobies call the
Galápagos home

Marine iguanas are
another local species

The Take Away

Wolf Volcano had not erupted in
more than 30 years, so I felt incredibly
lucky to have witnessed it. Even
more importantly, it was a once-in-a-
lifetime chance to see the geological
processes in action that have formed
the Galápagos – a huge privilege.

The Build Up

By far the most environmentally
responsible way to visit the Galápagos
is on a live-aboard boat, which includes
accommodation, activities inside the
national park, all meals and the services
of a qualified guide. By law, all visitors
to the Galápagos must follow a strict
itinerary that's been pre-approved
by the national park authority, and
be accompanied by an official park
naturalist at all times. For more rules

and regulations, consult The Galápagos
Conservancy (galapagos.org) or the Darwin
Foundation (darwinfoundation.org).

There are lots of vessels to choose from,
ranging in size from about 12 people up
to 100. Larger boats tend to have more
luxurious accommodation and facilities,
such as kayaks, diving gear and small
Zodiac dinghies. Visiting in low season from
April to May and September to October
is a good way to keep costs down, and
as boats prefer to travel full rather than
half-empty, it's possible to bag last-minute
deals if you're lucky. The Galápagos
Islands website (galapagosislands.com)
has links for recommended operators,
categorised according to budget.

Above: the Galápagos Islands' Wolf Volcano
only erupts once a generation

73

BIKING (AND BAGGING) MONT VENTOUX

PROVENCE, FRANCE

Jutting 1912m (6273ft) into the air and dominating the landscape in Provence, Mont Ventoux looks like a giant tumour – and this beast is anything but benign. Its quadricep-shredding roads have been the stage for plenty of drama in the Tour de France, including an episode that claimed the life of British cyclist Tom Simpson in 1967. The Tour is what first brought me to Ventoux in 2002. My then-husband and I were on a trip following the race, giving us the opportunity to cycle sections of the stages hours before the professionals tackled them. We tried to reach the summit on that sweltering July day, but we weren't fast enough to make it before officials closed the final few kilometres to recreational cyclists. Several years and one marriage later, I got my shot at redemption.

Staying at Crillon le Brave, set in the shadow of my mountainous tormentor, my second husband and I borrowed the hotel's bikes and – after cycling to the nearby town of Bedoin at the base of the climb – we granny-geared it up the long 21km (13 miles) to the top of Ventoux. At the lunar-like summit, we shared our lofty limestone perch with a few other sweaty cyclists who were beaming just like us, giddy with the same sense of accomplishment. I then noticed a man behind a long cart selling bins full of colourful sugary treats to cyclists. The symbolism wasn't lost on me. The day's success was all the sweeter knowing I tried and failed once before.

By Lori Rackl
Travel Editor, Chicago Tribune

The Take Away

Life can be stingy when it comes to doling out second chances. Getting back on a bike and finally bagging the summit of Mont Ventoux – one of the most epic climbs in cycling – felt incredible. Especially since this time, I got to do it with the true love of my life.

The Build Up

Cyclists have three ways to attack Mont Ventoux, from the towns Bedoin, Malaucene and Sault. The latter is considered the easiest of the trio largely because the climb, while a bit longer, isn't as steep in most places. The majority of bikers, however, prefer the classic route from Bedoin, a lively little village with several shops that rent road bikes (francebikerentals.com).

    The best time of year to cycle Ventoux is May to October. Be prepared to share the road with cars – and for weather to thwart your plans; winds sometimes get dangerously strong towards the top. A good base for a cycling adventure in this part of southeastern France is the hotel Crillon Le Brave, 40km (25 miles) northeast of Avignon (less than three hours from Paris on the high-speed TGV train). If you prefer to pedal with a group, Backroads offers two Provence cycling trips that include the option of biking Ventoux (backroads.com).

Left: announcing the approach to Mont
Ventoux's summit
Above: pedalling up the punishing ascent

74

LOST (AND FOUND) WITHOUT LANGUAGE OR DIRECTION

TIGER LEAPING GORGE, CHINA

After six hours of climbing blindly through the thicket of trees blanketing the mountainside, I was at a pretty low ebb. I had no idea where I was going or how long it would take. My guide – 16 years old with no English and a pale smile – was up ahead, climbing easily as though it were an afternoon stroll. My breath was getting shorter by the minute, my rucksack heavier and whatever sense of excitement I had at hiking Yunnan province's famous Tiger Leaping Gorge had long since disappeared in a fog of self-pity. I cursed my silent guide, China and the very idea of adventure travel.

Finally, just as I was about to give up altogether, the trees gave way to an open patch of grassland that dipped below the horizon a couple of hundred yards away. As I got to the grassy brow I could see the gorge laid out beneath me, the Jīnshā River a greeny-brown trickle 3900m (12,800ft) below the peaks of the mountains. All around me was untamed scenery, untouched and majestic. Tears welled up in my eyes and for one brief moment I felt as if I was in the presence of the divine. Suddenly, in the setting sun, the hardships of the past two days disappeared and the crippling uncertainty of feeling lost without language or direction was replaced by something altogether more powerful: the realisation that this moment was simply perfect.

By Fionn Davenport

The Take Away

I will never forget the feeling of sheer joy that came over me as I first caught a glimpse of the gorge below. Part of it was relief that the effort was worth it, but more than anything it was a recognition of beauty in its purest, natural form.

The Build Up

There is only one direct bus a day (leaving at 8.30am) from Lìjiāng's long-distance bus station to Qiáotóu, where the trek begins. However, you can hop on any bus to Shangri-La and then get off at Qiáotóu. Fares cost between ¥22 and ¥40 and the journey takes approximately 1½ hours.

A lot of the guesthouses in Lìjiāng can also arrange for a mini-van transfer to take you to the start of the trek – with the added bonus that they will deliver all the luggage you don't want to carry to the guesthouse of your choice along the route, usually Tina's (Zhōngxiá Lǚdiàn) or Jane's (Xiágǔ Xíng Kèzhàn), which are the most popular options for trekkers.

The trek itself is not easy, even if you're in decent shape, as the crumbling path is alarmingly narrow in places and requires great care and attention. Summer rainstorms can cause landslides and swollen waterfalls that can block the path, so check in Lìjiāng or Qiáotóu for trail and weather updates. Trail maps are good if not to scale, and be sure to bring plenty of water, sunscreen and lip balm.

Left: Tiger Leaping Gorge is 16km (10 miles) long and has a depth of 3900m (12,800ft)

75

ROAD-TRIPPING ON THE CARRETERA AUSTRAL

PATAGONIA, CHILE

From day one, Patagonia made me feel small. Ant-like. Nature loomed impossibly large, a wilderness painted in sweeping brush strokes on the vastest of canvases. The peaks of the Andes formed a gigantic ragged under-bite against the sky. The San Valentín glacier spread 2000m across and 100m high, groaning like an ogre and shedding chunks of ice the size of bungalows that hit Laguna San Rafael with a boom. I stood at the lip of a deep canyon, its roaring river a silent trickle far below, as condors cruised past me like bombers on a raid.

Through this epic wilderness snakes the Carretera Austral, the only road in and out of remotest southern Chile, and it's as untamed as the landscape around it. This rock-strewn track fights anything on its back, spitting stones and filling the air with thick plumes of dust. The occasional rusting skeleton of a car on the roadside bears testament to its lumps and potholes.

And for just a moment, as I drove high above a lake of impossible blue, the road took control. The back end of my vehicle slewed to the left, as though pushed by an invisible hand, the tyres skidding to the very edge of the sheer drop before something gripped and pulled me back to safety. I stopped to gather myself. All was now still. Sun pooled in the hollows of the mountains in the distance; the lake was like silk. I'd never felt smaller. And nature had never seemed so magnificent.

By Adrian Phillips
Managing Director, Bradt Travel Guides

The Take Away

Strange as it sounds, nothing is more liberating – exhilarating even – than to experience a true sense of insignificance. When the world is writ large, it provides context for the petty worries of life back home. In Patagonia, you're there on nature's terms, just a dot on the landscape.

The Build Up

The Carretera Austral – or Rte 7 – runs for almost 1250km through the southern half of Chile, from Puerto Montt to Villa O'Higgins.

Today, it has a fair claim to offering the world's most scenic road trip. Construction of the road began in the 1970s, and was only completed a decade or so ago. Until then, travel in this rural region of the country – characterised by glaciers, gorges, mountains and dense forest – was immensely difficult, and often the only practical means of access was via neighbouring Argentina. As such, the road is something of a lifeline for the sparse population here.

However, it's not an easy drive. While some portions are tarmacked,

much of the road is not, and there's a very real risk of an accident if you drive too quickly. The road can be travelled between November and March (with peak season January and February, when accommodation might be limited).

Be sure to request a 4WD when arranging your car hire. It's worth remembering that the rental cost is likely to be higher if the collection and drop-off points are different.

Left: the Carretera Austral rolls on through Chilean Patagonia

76

EPIPHANY AT NOTRE DAME

PARIS, FRANCE

After graduating from college, I lived in Paris for three months before beginning a one-year teaching fellowship in Greece. Footloose and purposeless, I was trying to figure out what to do with the rest of my life.

One afternoon I wandered into Notre Dame. At first I was overwhelmed by the vast stony hush, towering limestone arches and columns, and ethereal stained-glass windows. Then I saw a stone basin of water with a sign in seven languages: 'In the name of the father and the son and the Holy Spirit.' Illustrations showed a hand dipping into the water, then touching a forehead. Hesitantly I touched my hand to the cool, still water. As I brought wet fingers to my head, chills ran through my body and tears streamed into my eyes. Somehow that simple act had forged a palpable connection with the past: the fervent flow of pilgrims to the very stone on which I stood, the fervent procession of hands to water and fingers to forehead, all sharing this basin, this gesture.

I felt an electric sense of the history that flows within us and around us and beyond us – and I felt suffused with a new sense of purpose too. What would I do with my life? I would dip my fingers into the prayer water of human experience, all around the world. I would become a fervent pilgrim-writer, and I would bear witness to the sacred places, creations and encounters, the history and humanity, that connect us all.

By Don George

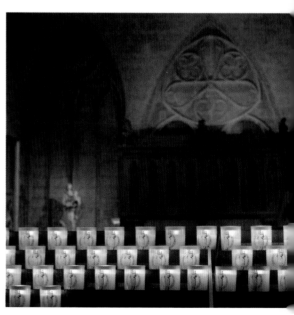

© Gianluca De Lorenzi | 500px, © Manjik Photography | 500px

The Take Away

After that moment, my life in Paris and later in Greece took on a new plan and purpose. I began writing feverishly in my journal, recording my impressions, experiences and lessons. Later I would translate these into articles – and become a travel writer and editor, which I have blessedly been ever since.

The Take Away

Notre Dame is one of the landmark sites in Paris, and as such it tends to be crowded any time of day. Especially in summer, queues can be dauntingly long. The cathedral is open from 7.45am to 6.45pm Monday to Friday and from 7.45pm to 7.15pm Saturday and Sunday. The best time to visit is first thing in the morning or around dusk. But whenever you visit, be sure to give yourself time to absorb the sacred spirit of the place. Too many tourists rush in and out. Walk in slowly, pause, look up and around, and open all your senses, not just to the soaring architecture and luminous stained-glass windows, but to the stony hush and musty scent of centuries, and to the floor stones rubbed smooth by countless soles. Sit in a pew and lose yourself to the cathedral's ancient, layered grace.

When you're properly enlightened and energised, repair across the plaza to the venerable restaurant Le Petit Chatelet; this is the perfect spot to sit at a sidewalk table, savour a wedge of roasted camembert on a crunchy baguette, and raise a glass of crisp rosé to the life-enlarging gift of this sacred space.

Above: the soaring heights of Notre Dame
Left: prayer candles burning with purpose

77

SUMMITING MT ELBRUS

RUSSIA

As the emergency helicopter set down in the small Inuit village on the west coast of Greenland, tears rolled down my cheeks, the sting of failure as painful as my injuries. I was being evacuated from the centre of Greenland's ice cap – the halfway point of our expedition – and my heart and mind longed for the feeling of success.

A year on and those feelings were again at the fore. I was at a point of exhaustion after 16 hours of climbing, and we were at a place on Mt Elbrus where we could get off, or push for the summit. Looking down, I could see an ominous storm rapidly rolling up the mountain, with lightning flashes getting closer and closer, yet a small gap in the weather above opened the door for a summit attempt. My heart was racing with nerves, but we pushed on.

The two hours that followed were extremely slow and heavy footed, and I was struggling to control my thoughts, emotions and body with each and every step up the ice face. My head was down and my muscles wanted me to stop, but it was the pain of failure in Greenland that kept me moving. The rising sun on the distant horizon briefly bathed my face in a positive warmth before the fierce storm and its blowing snow caught us just before the summit – it wasn't until I saw prayer flags around a small collection of stones that I knew we'd made it.

By Hugo Turner

© Hugo Turner

The Take Away

I used to think that failure reflected negatively on me, but now I look at it – and life – in a far more positive way. When something doesn't go to plan it provides you with learning opportunities and motivations for the future.

The Build Up

Less challenging to climb than Everest, but harder to summit than Kilimanjaro, Elbrus is similar to both in that its main routes are not technically challenging. However, it's recommended for climbers to have experience on ice, and it's a necessity to be in strong physical shape. A good local guide is also highly recommended.

Reaching the summit can be done in one long day, though it's highly recommended to spend at least a week acclimatising to the altitude before attempting the upper slopes. Most people with summit aspirations spend a few days in the villages of Terskol (2125m/6972ft) or Azau (2350m/7710ft) before using the lifts to access overnight sleeping options up the mountain to further their acclimatisation.

Summit attempts usually start from either Diesel Hut (4130m/13,550ft) or Pastukhov Rocks (4700m/15,420ft). From the former it's a 10- to 12-hour trek, while it's a seven- to eight-hour hike from the latter. Climbing season runs from late May to October. Permits are required for ascents above 3700m (12,140ft), and can be obtained from the Elbrus Area National Park Office.

Left: the storm follows Hugo and his brother up Mt Elbrus
Above: snow envelops the Turner twins at the summit

CHASING THE NORTHERN LIGHTS

LAPLAND, FINLAND

Snow crunched under my feet, an Arctic chill bore deep into my bones and adrenaline coursed through my veins. It was the dead of night, I was on a frozen river somewhere in Finnish Lapland and I was about to live out a long-held dream.

That night, as per the previous two, we had driven several hundred kilometres from the town of Ivalo, one eye on the road and the other fixed firmly skywards, until we scrambled down a snowy embankment onto the ice near the Russian border. My hopes were high after several failed attempts to see Mother Nature's finest performance in the skies of Iceland, Canada and Norway. But tonight it was quickly clear that the heavens were in the mood to put on a show.

We watched in silent wonder as the inky night sky came alive with emerald splashes, shimmering shapes, abstract angles and whimsical whirls that morphed with every passing second. It was thrilling, beautiful and glorious, and then it was gone.

We slowly headed back to the car but instinct made me stop. In a flash, the inky abyss exploded with a hundred shades of green, bold streaks tinged with red and sparks of sapphire. The aurora danced and twirled like a teenager. I sank into the thigh-high snow as I struggled to make sense of the ethereal beauty bearing down on me like icing sugar from a sieve. My heart thumped. My eyes streamed. My whole body quivered. And it had nothing to do with the cold.

By Nick Boulos

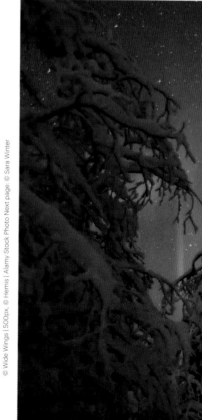

The Take Away

Years later, I still think about this moment. Did I imagine it? Did the aurora really move me to tears? Thankfully, I'm reminded every evening that it did. Hanging above my bed are some large prints of photographs that I captured on that magical Arctic night.

The Build Up

Best seen at latitudes above 35 degrees north between the months of October and March, the Northern Lights – or Aurora Borealis, to give the phenomenon its more scientific and poetic name – are formed by electronically charged particles colliding with the Earth's atmosphere around the Magnetic North Pole. The Aurora Australis is created in the same way around the South Magnetic Pole.

Catching either of these phenomena is a notoriously tricky business, with a number of factors at play. The conditions need to be perfect: a clear and crisp night, a place as far away as possible from light pollution and a splash of luck.

Experts suggest avoiding the months of November and December in northern Europe due to regular cloud cover. To truly maximise your chances, join a specialist trip that offers long hours and the possibility of travelling large distances to chase the lights.

Another piece of advice is to keep a close eye on the plane window during any night-time flights over the Arctic. Even on overcast nights, the aurora can sometimes be seen dancing happily above the clouds, oblivious to those below.

Left: heading north, away from any light polution
Below: the Aurora Borealis in all its colourful glory

GOLDEN CITY MORNINGS

SALAMANCA, SPAIN

The morning glow caught the steam from the café con leche as its wispy plumes dissipated into nothing. I tucked the small, crinkly package of sugar-encrusted magdalenas into my daypack, and listened to Moni's latest report about how she was rechoncha (chubby) and would spend her day at El Parque de los Jesuitas to lift her spirits. I just smiled, because I knew one of her pastimes was to smoke and clack through the park wearing her heels. I reassured Moni of her petite frame, kissed her cheek and stepped out to the clear and crisp morning.

I glided past the warm buttery-pastry shops and the butcher's storefront with dangling Salamanca jamón serrano. I rounded my last corner and step-hopped up the stairs through the damp, stone alleyway, which revealed Plaza Mayor.

Often the view following those Gothic arches slowed my gait, but on that particular day the glow drew me even closer. The sanguine rays danced across the ochre sandstone façade, and illuminated the proud red and gold flags. After glancing at the clock, I reluctantly kept walking, following the diagonal shadow that cut across the breadth of the plaza's court.

Out from the other side stood a small pastelería where I rarely skipped indulging in its flaky croissants. I asked about the baker's daughters and said my second goodbye of the morning. I took a bite from my fresh pastry, and strolled on to class, admiring the stunning golden landmarks that had become my home.

By Kait Reynolds

Salamanca's 16th-century Casa de las Conchas

The Take Away

In one fleeting summer my world changed: Moni became my Spanish mom, I walked to school with a newfound curiosity, and I achieved my dream of becoming fluent in Spanish. And I surprised myself, not because I fell in love with Spain, but because my new perspectives breathed life into everything mundane.

The Build Up

Direct trains are available from Madrid's Chamartín station to Salamanca, and they run four times per day. In less than two hours you'll arrive at Salamanca's La Alamedilla station, a 10-minute walk away from Plaza Mayor. Begin by passing Parque de la Alamedilla, following signs towards the old city. Take a left, and ramble along Calle Azafranal, which leads directly to Plaza Mayor.

Continue your journey towards the plaza's southwest corner. There you'll find a scallop shell trail marker for the Camino de Santiago. Stroll past this, and take an immediate left, which leads towards La Universidad de Salamanca, and La Plaza de Anaya, where the elusive Rana de Salamanca hides in the

façade's carvings. If you walk just a little further, peruse Catedral de Salamanca with scrutiny in order to find the hidden astronaut preserved in the stone entrance.

Salamanca is as traditional a Spanish town as it is stunning. The weekends here are slower, with fewer businesses open, and between 2pm and 5pm most stores are closed for siesta. So take in the sights in the best morning light, grab some rest during siesta, and join Salamancans for *pinchos* (tapas-like snacks) in the radiant Plaza Mayor.

Top: Plaza Mayor, the old town's radiant hub
Above: snack on platters of local Jamón serrano

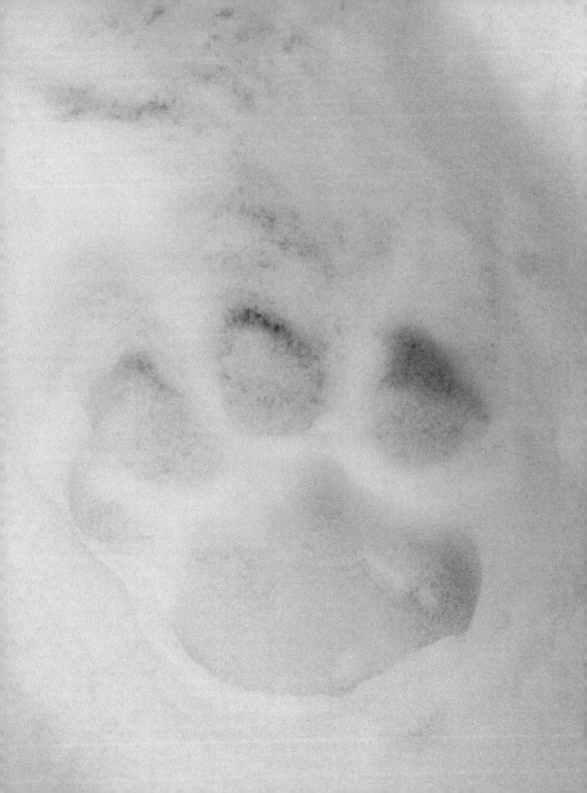

TRACKING SNOW LEOPARDS

LADAKH, INDIA

We'd been searching for three days, venturing out each morning from our tiny homestay and returning by evening to thaw out beside the fire. Fresh snowfall had limited our wanderings – at 3800m (12,500ft) altitude and 20°C below zero, the going was tough. But it also made a blank canvas of the rugged landscape on which any passing snow leopard would write its signature. Norbu, our guide, was on the case, scrutinising the slopes for tracks while we watched ibex crest the ridges and golden eagles spiral into the blue.

I've always liked big cats. Who doesn't? But snow leopards hold a particular allure. Perhaps it was that childhood zoo encounter, watching the caged beast relentlessly pacing its imagined mountains until my parents dragged me away. Or reading Peter Matthiessen's travel classic,

in which six months of combing Tibet for the eponymous animal produced not a single glimpse. Just the name seems to embody the unobtainable. Snow. Leopard. Like something from Narnia.

It was the ibex that gave the game away: a panicked gallop across a gully then a collective stare back towards the boulder field. We stared with them, willing the predator to appear. 'Shan,' breathed Norbu. And suddenly into my binocular field walked that tell-tale profile: all prowling, feline grace; the improbably enormous tail swinging behind. Two fluid bounds and it was up onto a ledge. Too far for photos. Nonetheless, we watched and waited – until the clouds rolled in and the mountains reclaimed their secret.

By Mike Unwin

The Take Away

I learned that the power of a wildlife encounter is in its context, not its photo ops. My sighting may have been distant but its thrill lay in the cold, the exhaustion and the intimidating vastness of the Himalayas. It was a stirring reminder that some places still remain beyond our clutches.

The Build Up

Snow leopards range across some 1.5 million sq km of central Asia but with fewer than 7500 individuals left they are elusive. Your best chance is on a small-group, guided tour. Ladakh is a hot spot – particularly

in and around Hemis National Park, where the animals receive protection and tour companies work closely with the community.

The tracking season is November–April, when the cats follow their prey to lower altitudes. April's courting season is especially productive.

If arriving from overseas, your tour will likely incorporate 2–3 nights' acclimatisation in Leh (Ladakh's capital). You'll then continue into the mountains where, from a community homestay, you'll explore on foot and by vehicle with local guides. Accommodation is comfortable but the altitude, terrain and cold can be demanding.

Sightings are never guaranteed but there is plentiful other wildlife, including blue sheep, ibex, wolves and mountain birds. You'll also experience Buddhist culture and gawp at the world's greatest mountains.

Operators include Steppes Travel (steppestravel.com), Naturetrek (naturetrek.co.uk) and Natural World Safaris (naturalworldsafaris. com). Tours start at around £3000. You can also track snow leopards in Bhutan, Pakistan, Nepal and, at lower altitudes, Mongolia.

Left: following in the footsteps of the elusive snow leopard

81

A Hindu sadhu, or holy person, at Haridwar

THE GREAT HINDU GATHERING

HARIDWAR, INDIA

As the Kumbh Mela gathering reached a cosmic alignment of chaos and cacophony, the Hindustan Times was reporting 14 million pilgrims already inside the city and 100,000 arriving every hour. So when I stepped outside my hotel I was buffeted along by a maelstrom of pilgrims seeking quick karma via an auspicious snan (bath) in the sacred Ganges. Hundreds and thousands were on the move: flowing like a river in spate towards Har-ki-Pairi Ghat, where Hindu mythology claims the amrit (nectar) of immortality was dropped down from heaven via Vishnu.

Immovable holy cows proved decorated impediments to the febrile crowd. The fug of marijuana exhaled by orange-robed ascetics mingled with sweeter aromas of sandalwood and incense. One long-haired pilgrim waving Shiva's trident smeared vermilion kumkum on my forehead and grinned maniacally. I told myself to just stay upright and stay alive in the crush. But actually I'd never felt more alive, cheek-by-jowl with the ecstasy of belief that there was life beyond mortality.

We poured over the stone ghat steps into the Ganges, as if a waterfall. Borne by momentum my karma was cast in Har-ki-Pairi's ancient sacred stones. I joined pilgrims in stripping down to underwear then splashed, howling with cold and laughing hysterically, into glacial waters that funnelled down from the Himalayas. I'd never felt so exhilarated. The devotional chant of Har Har Mahadev burrowed into my brain as a cup of sweet Indian chai revived my chilled extremities. The greatest show on Earth had held me in its throes.

By Mark Stratton

© Mark Stratton

One pilgrim collects alms prior to aarti worship

The Take Away

Besides generating overwhelming emotions, this experience also imbued in me a new sense of self-confidence that I could thrive in any adversity – I'd lived off my instincts and survived the intense and mind-altering melee. I also felt honoured to better understand a religion that to outsiders can seem baffling.

The Build Up

Determined by the cosmic alignment of the heavens, Kumbh Melas occur four times over a 12-year cycle at Haridwar, Prayag (Allahabad), Nashik and Ujjain. The next full Kumbh Mela returns to Haridwar in 2022. This experience is probably not one for first-time visitors to India – spend a week in Varanasi first to see if you can cope with the cultural complexities (and also the heat if the mela occurs during summer).

Plan at least one year in advance; the issue isn't flights to India but getting to the city and accommodation once there. You can book a train to Haridwar from Delhi online via Indian Railways (indianrail.gov. in) some months in advance. Excellent options for accommodation are the purpose-built tented camps that you can arrange via specialist tour operators such as Transindus (transindus.co.uk). Given the scale of the Kumbh Mela and your close proximity to millions of revellers, make sure your inoculations are updated because good karma doesn't guarantee immortality. Claustrophobics need not apply.

Below: *crowds descend to bathe in the Ganges*

EYES OVER THE OUTBACK

RED CENTRE, AUSTRALIA

Struggling to contain my excitement, I laid the wing of my paramotor out on the hot Australian sand. I was about to attempt to fly 30km (19 miles) south to Mt Connor (859m/2818ft), a distinctive flat-topped monolith rising dramatically out of Australia's Northern Territory – it was a flight I'd always longed to do.

With safety checks complete and the engine warmed up, I raised the wing above me. Glowing in the late-afternoon winter sun, my paramotor was ready for take off. I was soon airborne, and conditions were perfect – a slight tailwind was propelling me towards my lofty goal. I could feel the smooth, cold air on my bare legs (wearing shorts allows me to feel the different air pressures, and enables me to avoid the more turbulent hot layers of air) as the sun started to near the western horizon.

However, it became apparent that the quickly fading light wouldn't allow me to reach Mt Connor, so I made a sweeping turn to aim back towards base. And then it hit me – soaring majestically out of Australia's Red Centre, some 120km (75 miles) away, were Uluru and Kata Tjuta. I couldn't quite believe the scale of the view that welcomed me. And the combination of desert dust and the sun's last light was turning everything the most astonishing orange.

By Ross Turner

The Take Away

I'd been so focused on getting to Mt Connor that I hadn't bothered to notice what was around me. Sometimes you have to lift your head up and relish the journey instead of solely concentrating on the destination. I now make sure I take moments to pause, reflect and take everything in.

The Build Up

To fly a paramotor (powered paraglider; PPG) in Australia and elsewhere, it's necessary to get a PPG licence via the Association of Paragliding Pilots and Instructors (appippg.org). These can be acquired after an intensive training course and building up your flight hours.

For such an expedition in the Northern Territory you'd also need to bring plenty of kit besides the paramotors themselves, namely reserve wings, helmets, satellite phones, GPS tracker, solar panels, camping gear, fuel, food and water. Time is also needed to research local air restrictions, flight paths of commercial planes, emergency routes and roads, weather systems and patterns, and thermal forecasts – all of which are crucial in determining your flight path.

Mt Connor has significant meaning to the Aboriginal people of Australia, who know it as Atila. Often mistaken for Uluru, it can be seen from the Lasseter Hwy, which connects Uluru-Kata Tjuta National Park with Alice Springs via the Stuart Hwy. You'll see a well-signposted lookout about 20km (12 miles) east of Curtin Springs.

Left: looking down over Uluru and the great expanse of the Red Centre

83

UNLIKELY ENCOUNTER ON THE THAMES

LONDON, ENGLAND

It was a raw March afternoon, and I was perched over the cold waters of the River Thames on an unstable stand-up paddleboard (SUP). It was my first solo SUP journey, and my plan was to head upriver from Kew Bridge with the current and then turn back when the tide changed. I made good time, so I kept paddling to Teddington Lock, which marks the end of the tidal Thames. As I started to return I noticed a big column of gulls wheeling around in the grey air at the southern tip of Eel Pie Island. I was bemused until I noticed a black head bob up from the murky water just below them.

For a second, I thought it was someone in a silicone swim cap, but swimmers, even cold water ones, don't usually have a big green tench dangling from their mouths. It was a seal! Judging by the shape of her head, a young female harbour seal. I couldn't believe my luck. She munched her fish for a while, then slipped silently under the surface. The gulls tracked her downriver, as did I, paddling hard on my knees for 20 minutes until our game of peekaboo ended in the depths. Seeing her this far up the Thames, knowing all the bridges and traffic

she'd negotiated, I knew I was witnessing a triumphant act of defiance. And given the river was declared biologically dead in 1957, I was also filled with a great feeling of hopefulness.

By Marcel Theroux

Standing steady on an SUP takes study and balance

The River Thames at
Teddington

The Take Away

What stays with me is a sense of unexpectedness that bordered on magic. It also reminded me of a Faroese folk tale about a seal who takes human form. While ending sadly, it speaks to the kinship between humans and seals, the uncanny feeling that we're part of the same biological family.

The Take Away

Stand-up paddleboarding is one of the fastest growing sports in the world, with an ever-increasing array of schools and rentals cropping up by most bodies of water. In southwest London, Active 360 Paddleboarding (active360.co.uk) offers SUP rentals (£20 for two hours), beginner lessons (from £57) and organised trips (£22) on the Thames from its base at Kew Bridge – depending on the tides, you can either head upriver towards Richmond or downriver towards Hammersmith. The company also has options on the Thames at Putney, along Brentford Lock (where the River Brent joins the Grand Union Canal) and in Paddington Basin (near the junction of Regents Canal and the Grand Junction Canal).

While it's possible to hire SUPs at Paddington by demonstrating your manoeuvring skills, at the other locations you must complete at least a lesson before it's even an option to go out on your own. On the east side of London, based out of the Western Beach in the Royal Victoria Dock, is Wakeup Docklands (wakeupdocklands. com) – between May and October it offers one-hour 'taster' lessons for £30 or two-hour 'qualifying' options (£50); the latter gain you some independence.

Above: a playful and ever-inquisitive harbour seal

84

FOLLOW ME: JAPANESE HOSPITALITY

HIDA-FURUKAWA, JAPAN

I still remember the excitement I felt opening the invitation – Japan had always been on my wish list, and the wedding coincided with both the cherry blossom season and the famous spring festival of Takayama Matsuri.

Months later, the sakura burst into colour on the wedding day and the ceremony was, in a word, perfect. Unsurprisingly, I was on an incredible high – I'd seen close friends tie the knot, and I'd had a wonderfully remarkable 10 days exploring the country. Only one dream left: Takayama Matsuri.

At the last minute that dream turned to a nightmare when I realised my hotel booked online wasn't within a day's reach of the festival, and there were no vacancies anywhere in Takayama. In a panic, I travelled to Hida-Furukawa, the next major train stop outside the city. Hungry and stressed, I arrived the day before the festival, managed to find a small hotel and stopped for some sushi. The chef, realising I was English, woke up his wife to translate my order (I was mortified!). But she sat with me and happily chatted at length. Not content for me to explore alone in the rainy darkness, she grabbed an umbrella after I was done eating and gestured for me to follow. In next few hours we took in a children's traditional music recital, a sake brewery, three temples and a shrine, a beautiful bridge, trees laden with blossom, winding streets and canals laden with koi. She then invited me for a second meal at home with her family.

By Katharine Nelson

The Take Away

Travellers are sometimes exposed to beautiful human impulses and experience unthinkable hospitality. This family shared their lives (and town) with me, turning a night I was dreading into one I ended up cherishing. And my last-minute hotel was the most wonderfully traditional of the entire trip. Travel always has the power to surprise.

The Build Up

Japan's innumerable cherry trees burst into life each spring, and their blossoms blanket streetsides, hills and parks in shades of white and pink – it's a sight to behold, and many people travel at this time of year. The exact timing of the blossoms is impossible to predict, but the season tends to climax between 25 March and 7 April around Takayama (as well as Tokyo and Kyoto).

On the other hand, Takayama Matsuri – one of the country's greatest festivals – erupts like clockwork twice a year. The largest version (Sannō Matsuri) takes place on 14 and 15 April, while the smaller edition (Hachiman Matsuri) is on 9–10 October. The colourful event features parades of incredibly ornate, multi-tiered *yatai* (floats) that are festooned with dolls, carvings, curtains and lanterns. The entire event is accompanied by sacred music.

If you miss the festival, view a few *yatai*, some of which date to the 17th century, in the Takayama Festival Floats Exhibition Hall.

Takayama is connected by frequent *shinkansen* (bullet train) service to Nagoya, which can be combined with the JR Takayama line to reach Tokyo (¥5510, 2½ hours). Little Hida-Furukawa is three stops north of Takayama on a local train (¥240, 15 minutes).

Left: a float at the Takayama Matsuri parade
Above: Japanese cherry tree in full blossom

85

CAREFREE CAMPERVAN ADVENTURE

ISLE OF LEWIS, OUTER HEBRIDES, SCOTLAND

Below: not a soul on the sand of this beach on the Isle of Lewis

We had no fixed destination, and that was the beauty of it. My boyfriend and I had swapped our comfy London bed for a VW campervan, and had shoved our precious belongings – pillows, puffer jackets and tea bags – into its boot and cabinets. We took the first single-track road (it didn't matter which one), turned the music up and drove alongside fields of golden heather, stopping occasionally to let snoozing sheep saunter off the road and slowing to snap pictures of scarecrows cloaked in high-vis jackets.

Then we rounded a corner and saw it. There, in front of us, on the rough and remote Outer Hebridean island of Lewis, was the most dazzling sweep of cream sand, its far edge lapped with small fluoro-green waves, its sides flanked by steel-grey rock. We slammed to a halt, kicked off our trainers and ran to the freezing water – our footsteps the only marks on the sand, our feet the first to touch the North Atlantic that day.

The beach felt impossible to leave behind, and so we didn't. We parked up on a patch of grass and guzzled cans of strong beer until a cyan sky slid into a dusty magenta and eventually to a star-studded black. No lights, no traffic, no mobile-phone reception. No worries, no hassle, no stress. And refreshingly, no people. That night we fell asleep to the sound of the wind skimming the water, of waves falling onto the sand. The next morning? A brew with a view – one I'll never forget.

By Hannah Summers

The Take Away

It turns out that some of the world's best beaches scatter the British coastline I've always felt so desperate to leave behind. Every day I crave the simplicity, freedom and flexibility of living in that van, and our 24 hours parked up on that remote beach near the tiny village of Bhaltos.

The Build Up

Campervan holidays are becoming increasingly popular in the UK, with a flurry of a new websites offering short- and long-term rentals. Try quirkycampers.co.uk, which provides hand-crafted campers located in London, Bristol and Scotland.

Ferries to the Isle of Lewis depart from Ullapool, on the northwest coast of Scotland, a 4½ hour drive from Glasgow.

Take a morning crossing and you'll arrive in Stornoway, the island's capital, 2½ hours later (book online in advance through calmac.co.uk to find the best price).

Responsible wild camping is legal in most of Scotland, meaning you don't need to book campsites – simply find a suitable spot and politely settle in. The tiny community-owned village of Bhaltos can be reached by heading west from Stornoway on the A858, before heading south at Garrynahine on the B80011. Eventually take the turning north signposted Cnip. You'll know the beach when you see it. There are no shops, petrol stations or lights on this part of the Isle of Lewis – you will need to buy your supplies and fill up in Stornoway, and be sure to have enough water on board to last, along with camping essentials including torches.

86

THE ULTIMA THULE EVEREST EXPEDITION

MOUNT EVEREST, TIBET

Photographing a mountain landscape is about much more than just the physical elements, it's about capturing the experience of being there: the magic of the light, the thin, sharp cold of the air, the altitude and its effects on your body, the mood you sensed when you first saw the composition you wanted to capture.

In the early 1980s I was invited to be the photographer for the Seattle-based Ultima Thule Everest Expedition. We were the first Western team permitted to attempt to climb the famed Northeast Ridge since George Mallory and Andrew Irvine disappeared on it in 1924.

On 27 March 1984, we arrived in Lhasa and travelled through increasingly remote villages and finally to Everest base camp. For three months our team tried to get a man on the summit – two nearly succeeded, failing by less than 250m (800ft). Plagued by bad weather, illness and the departure of high-altitude porters, we ran out of time. According to our Chinese climbing permit, we had to be off the mountain and out of China by 5 June or face a US$50,000 penalty. We had no choice but to descend, though for three months we had participated in a grand adventure, among the highest, most spectacular mountains on Earth.

By Art Wolfe

The Take Away

Remote mountain peaks touch us in a way that other environments can't. It's human nature to want to get to the top of things, to be the highest, to challenge our very limits. People dream, obsess and risk their lives to summit, whether it's Mount Everest or a volcanic peak in the Cascade Range. This expedition has resonated through my life like no other. Can a moment last months, even years? I think so.

The Build Up

Although there are more than 18 named routes up Everest, some of which have still not been successfully completed, the Northeast Ridge is one of the two main options, along with the South Col route. The latter gives climbers the possibility of a helicopter rescue at base camp, as well as warmer temperatures and less wind, though it does come with risks: the Khumbu Icefall and a long push to the summit, which can be worsened by crowding.

The Northeast Ridge is exposed to more severe weather, its camp locations are at more testing elevations and the climbing is more difficult. But it does offer a shorter push to the peak on summit night. Take your pick.

Tibet is open to outsiders, but the Chinese government maintains stringent control over visitors in this autonomous region – before booking a plane ticket from home, or train tickets from Beijing to the Lhasa, you must apply for a Tibet Tourism Bureau (TTB) permit from a registered tour company or agency. Note that travel outside Lhasa also requires an additional Aliens' Travel Permit (ATP), issued by the Public Security Bureau. You need to decide on your itinerary before applying. Independent travel is not permitted.

Left: the Ultima Thule Everest Expedition, backed by the North Face

87

LEARNING TO LOVE SOLITUDE

MENDOZA, ARGENTINA

'You emerge from this marvellous novel as if from a dream, the mind on fire...' the back-cover review by New York Times *journalist John Leonard could not have been more apt.*

I was sitting outside a café sipping an early-evening glass of deep, rich, fruity Malbec. Sycamore leaves flitted across a wide pavement still warm from the gentle late summer sun. A plate of empanadas sat on the table, each a little warm and flaky pastry parcel of beef, chicken or cheese. And next to them lay a yellowed, second-hand copy of One Hundred Years of Solitude by Gabriel García Márquez.

I'd bought it from a bookseller under Waterloo Bridge years before, but had never even opened the cover. But now I had time: ill health and bereavement had forced an abrupt, six-month sabbatical from work. Yet through a fog of grief and despair I'd found the courage to book a ticket around the world, beginning in Argentina but with little idea of where to go or what to do.

For no other reason than Malbec being my favourite wine, I grabbed an overnight bus to Mendoza when I landed in Buenos Aires. As I lay in my seat watching a spectacular electrical storm light up the 2am sky over the Pampas, tears rolled down my tired cheeks. In London I'd

been too scared to do anything alone – did I now have the courage to travel solo for six months?

Then, suddenly, unexpectedly, on that warm pavement in Mendoza, I was alone and at peace.

By Abigail Butcher

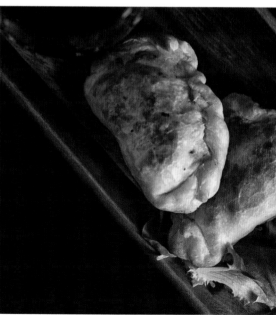

© Columbo photog. © Edsel Querini

The Take Away

Looking back conjures a feeling of utter contentment. I felt awake, alive and empowered for the first time in years. The simple act of ordering those empanadas, drinking a glass of Malbec and reading the most evocative book of my life, changed everything – it gave me the courage to go forward.

The Build Up

Mendoza is in the heart of Argentina's wine country and is one of the country's finest cities. Set 1050km (652 miles) west of Buenos Aires, life here centres on plazas and outdoor cafes, beneath rows of huge sycamore trees.

Close to the border with Chile, Mendoza is in the foothills of the Andes, which supply it with a backdrop of the most spectacular scenery as well as snowmelt that trickles down open *acequias* (irrigation channels) along the wide, leafy streets.

The irrigation channels also provide life to the vineyards. Some 70% of Argentina's wine is produced here, and as well as sampling the various grapes (Syrah, Cabernet and Chardonnay in addition to the glorious Malbec) in cafes, bars and restaurants, you can take walking, cycling or hop-on, hop-off bus tours of the many wine producers in the area.

The best way to travel from Buenos Aires to Mendoza, if you have the time, is by using Argentina's comfortable and affordable bus system – journey times vary between 13 and 18 hours, with tickets starting from AR$950 (omnilineas.com). Numerous daily flights also connect the two cities.

Above: the vineyards of Mendoza at the foot of the Andes
Left: lamb-stuffed empanadas to accompany a glass of Malbec

88

GUYANA'S GREATEST GIFT

KAIETEUR NATIONAL PARK, GUYANA

A rush of anticipation had surged through me long before arrival. To fly southwest across Guyana is to enter the South America of wild imagination, where the urban din of Georgetown, the capital of this small country on the northeast shoulder of the continent, is replaced, almost instantly, by a blur of green rainforest, swelling below the plane's wings.

I knew I was visiting the sort of location that Victorian explorers spent decades seeking, but the fantasy could not have prepared me for the reality. Kaieteur Falls could be a blueprint, divinely drawn, for a jungle waterfall. Though less forceful than Iguazú Falls, and shorter than Salto Ángel, it has a purity of purpose making it greater than either – the planet's longest single-drop cascade,

where the Potaro River plunges 226m (741ft).

I could hear it before I saw it; first it was a whisper, then a gasp, and finally a roar. And suddenly, there it was before me, a masterpiece – the river smooth like marble on approach, then tumbling down into a cloud of mist. I flattened onto my stomach on the edge of the chasm and stared down. Because I could. Nobody else was present beyond our party of five, and there were no railings, no rules.

Kaieteur Falls is named after Kai, an Amerindian chief who reputedly paddled into the abyss to please the gods. Lying there, hypnotised by the torrent's seductive call, I could, for one mad moment, grasp the lure of such sacrifice.

By Chris Leadbeater

The Take Away

Espying Kaieteur Falls in such isolation was an episode that never left me. It is the hour by which I now measure all other travel experiences. The thrill was further amplified by the departing flight, which took off directly over the falls for an amazing view.

The Build Up

Kaieteur National Park's remoteness is underscored by the fact that, although the Guyana Tourism Authority considers it the most popular attraction in the country, the record year for footfall (2012) witnessed a mere 6667 visitors. The issue is one of access. Realistically, you need a guide and a pre-arranged tour to reach the area. Guyana's official tourist site (exploreguyana.org) requests that interested parties 'plan and book your tour to Kaieteur with a recognised tour company', and offers a few suggestions.

One of these is Wilderness Explorers (wilderness-explorers. com), a respected operator that has worked in Guyana since 1994. Most of its itineraries call at Kaieteur Falls, and are generally a fly-in day-trip from Georgetown.

For the more active traveller, the company offers the energetic alternative of an eight-day 'Kaieteur Overland' jaunt, which tiptoes towards the Falls via 4WD, boat and hiking boot.

Left: Guyana's Kaieteur Falls plunge 226m (741ft)

89

Mark driving his Land Rover through the wilds of Kidepo Valley National Park

FACE TO FACE WITH SEVEN LIONS

KIDEPO VALLEY NATIONAL PARK, UGANDA

It was mid-afternoon and I was battling siesta-hour drowsiness under the hot equatorial sun. My feet were up on the bumper of the Land Rover, and I'd had my head down in my laptop screen for well over an hour. I knew there were hypnotic views down to the shimmering plains, but I was in Kidepo Valley National Park as a volunteer, and I needed to get map data uploaded if I had any chance of exploring the area that afternoon.

Suddenly a harsh cough broke my concentration, like claws slashing a mosquito net, and I instinctively looked up to find myself staring straight into the amber eyes of a lion. It was less than 50m (160ft) away, and after a quick scan of the granite outcrops, I realised it was not alone... there were six others.

Yet, given their relaxed, lazy-looking state – paws coyly crossed – I didn't make a dash for it. That would have felt rather melodramatic as they'd clearly been there a while. Instead I slowly sidled around the Land Rover to ease the door open for a bolthole. I then aimed a hissed whisper over my shoulder towards the tents where my three teammates were dozing: 'Hey guys... some visitors here you might want to meet...'

The lions remained at ease even when we started barbecuing sausages as dusk fell, though they must have been hungry as I was woken that evening by the bellowing of a panicked buffalo being taken down by this Kidepo pride.

By Mark Eveleigh

© Mark Eveleigh

The Take Away

I realised that I was too often oblivious to life's dramas happening around me. Here I'd not only been blind to the beauty of Africa's most spectacular national park, but I'd allowed an entire pride of lions to walk up to me unnoticed. Looking up is never a bad idea!

The Build Up

Tucked into Uganda's far northeastern corner, Kidepo Valley National Park remains one of Africa's hidden wildernesses. These spectacular plains and valleys cover an area that is only slightly smaller than Greater London. Yet you're a long way from traffic jams here; in fact, it's rare to see another vehicle. That said, Kidepo can get spectacularly congested with herds of elephants, antelope, zebra and marauding lions. The park is also home to 500 bird species and 86 species of mammal, 28 of which can be found nowhere else in the country. Herds of more than 4000 buffalo often seem to stretch right across the valley to the foothills of Morungole, the sacred mountain of the mysterious Ik tribe.

Kidepo's isolated position, wedged between South Sudan and Kenya's Turkana region, means most visitors opt for a charter flight here rather than the 12-hour road-trip from Entebbe international airport. Either way, it's an adventure, and the remoteness is what makes Kidepo so exciting. Stay at the luxurious Apoka Safari Lodge (wildplacesafrica.com; US$1170 for an all-inclusive double) or the more affordable Uganda Wildlife Authority *bandas* (ugandawildlife.org; doubles from US$15).

Below: one of the lions that were rather interested in Mark and his camp

LIFE LESSONS IN THE AMAZON

RIO URUBU, BRAZIL

It was day four of our multi-year honeymoon, and we were in a dugout canoe in the middle of the Amazon jungle with a hammock, machete and some fishing line. As we paddled through the black waters of the Urubu River, our guide Cristóvão pointed to the rippling waters. 'Piranhas,' he said. Just as I was ready to paddle backwards, he took a strong stroke towards the famed flesh-eaters.

He dropped in a baited line and it wasn't long before the piranhas hooked onto the waiting morsels. Cristóvão immediately slung out the line and two maniacal piranhas landed onto the floor of the boat. My trembling knees shot to my chest, before he quickly (and calmly) knocked them out with the butt of his machete. Victorious, he smiled at me and said, 'Ana... your turn.'

I realised that as much as we had tried to prepare for our round-the-world trip (and even for this particular voyage into the depths of the Amazon), we were clueless. Cristóvão, on the other hand, was born and raised in the Amazon and his every move through the rainforest seemed effortless – building a shelter from palm leaves, whittling a blow dart gun, foraging for fruits and navigating the unknown. His life was completely different from ours back in the States, and clearly we had so much to learn from him.

By Anne Howard

© Anne Howard

The Take Away

In our five days together with Cristóvão, he taught us to adapt to our environment, to be resourceful and to find patience. At the time we thought he was teaching us how to survive in the jungle... but we later realised those lessons were actually preparing us for our journey through life.

The Build Up

Manaus, the gateway into this Amazon experience, is best reached via plane or boat. Flights arrive into Aeroporto Internacional Eduardo Gomes, which is 13km (8 miles) north of the city centre. Large passenger boats link the city with Tabatinga (7 days; from R$350) upstream and with Belém (4 days; R$300), the capital of the state of Pará, downstream. Smaller, somewhat comfortable speed boats can halve the journey times, though they cost almost double.

Once in Manaus, navigate your way to the family run Amazonas Indian Turismo (311 Dos Andradas St). If you're lucky, its founder Soares will be behind the desk – though don't be alarmed if he interrupts his trip description to shoot a blow dart across the room. The family's home on the Rio Urubu, which is comprised of open-walled thatch structures and a wooden outhouse (don't expect running water or electricity), will be your base between overnight excursions. Hiking and canoeing will bring you to remote parts of the jungle, where you will set up camps of palm-leaf shelters and hammocks.

Guides speak English and are incredibly knowledgeable about the jungle and its practical and cultural uses.

Above: Anne building a shelter in the Amazon with her guide Cristóvão
Left: Cristóvão paddling through the piranha-filled waters

91

A MOUNTAIN GAZELLE

YEMEN

I was in Sana'a, Yemen's capital, and it was fascinating but I kept looking out of windows at the desert in the distance thinking of Freya Stark who followed ancient frankincense trade routes in the 1930s. My host said, 'Let me see what I can do.'

At dawn the next day we were on the road to the Ramlat al Sabatein desert, heading to the fabled ruined city of Shabwa, capital of the Hadhramaut. Under armed protection, I was hidden under a black abaya (traditional cloak) and it was like a pantomime, although the AK-47s looked real enough.

On the road I was happy: enormous sky, Bedouin camps, camel trains and sand dunes, but soon we were stopped, officials took our passports and the atmosphere changed. I walked away from the car and the tension, light with fear in this place where kidnapping was frequent.

Looking down into the valley I realised that I was being watched by a creature with elegantly curved antlers and a pattern on the inside of the ears similar to the veined skeleton of a leaf. It was a mountain gazelle, as fragile and vulnerable as me. As I was watching its immense beauty, while standing alone in this vast, wide landscape, I felt less afraid.

My friend called. 'We aren't allowed,' he said, gesturing me back into the car. We turned back. 'Freya Stark didn't make it there, either,'

I said, 'but she was still glad she came.'

As we pulled away, the gazelle didn't run, it watched us. I knew then that life involved courage and movement, not just staying in safe boxes. The key was to not run away and hide but to trust as the gazelle had trusted me.

By Suzanne Joinson

The Take Away

Despite the edginess of being vulnerable, the mountain gazelle trusting me was the loveliest gift the desert could have given me. A reminder that there is magic in the world and that to shut oneself up in the name of safety does not work. On my last night in Yemen we made a toast to the roads we want to take, the ones we do take and the ones we are destined only to imagine. I finally understood the balance between being both vulnerable and brave.

The Take Away

Exploring Yemen is sadly not advisable in its current state of security, with conflict and terrorism leading to the most stringent of travel advisories blanketing the entire country since March 2011. Commercial flights in and out of the country are non-existent, with planes working on humanitarian efforts being the only ones able to operate (albeit under strict restrictions). Travel by road is currently no better and many routes are often being closed or blocked.

When the security situation improves, visitors should again be able to enjoy Yemen's vast desert and mountain landscapes, incredible architecture and some of the most hospitable and friendly people on the planet. Don't be surprised by sincere invitations into their homes, for a meal, Yemeni coffee or just a warm-hearted conversation.

You'll find its capital's streets alive with the melodic calls to prayer, songs of street sellers and traditional Yemeni *oud* rhythms. Here, markets such as Nogom Central and the historic Souq al-Melh burst with energy and are filled with the pungent aroma of spices and wares of endless variety.

Above: a mountain gazelle
Left: Sana'a, Yemen's capital, before the war

92

A TRUE TRANSITION IN TRANSIT

NARITA, JAPAN

I was reeling from my first trip ever to Southeast Asia – Thailand, Burma, Hong Kong and Macao – and hungry to get back to my flat in New York City; the last thing I wanted was a 20-hour layover at Narita Airport near Tokyo.

But that was what my itinerary called for, so I took a shuttle bus upon arrival to the Hotel Nikko Narita and wondered how I could kill the remaining hours. The next morning I saw a sign for a free shuttle into the town of Narita, and since I was sure I'd never be back in Japan, I jumped on. Twenty minutes later, I was walking through narrow lanes of wooden houses up to a 1000-year-old temple. It was a brilliant day in late October, radiant with the

first colours of autumn, but tinged with the first mildness of the coming dark and cold.

I didn't know then that Narita's temple is a celebrated pilgrimage site and that the faithful sometimes walk almost 75km (46 miles) from central Tokyo to visit its prayer halls and garden. I simply knew that the intimate scale of things – from the tatami mats to the day's mingled feelings – felt, for reasons I couldn't explain, like a home I'd been looking for all my life. By the time I boarded my plane in the early afternoon, I'd decided to move to Japan. I've been here now for more than 30 years.

By Pico Iyer

The Take Away

Decades of constant travel have shown me that it's often the ordinary places that move one more than the iconic sites ever do; nearly always it's those not even on the itinerary that turn one's life around. But I've never had such dramatic evidence as in the unsought transit that redirected me forever.

The Build Up

With as little as a five-hour layover at Narita International Airport, you shall have enough time to explore

Narita town and enjoy a meal before heading back for your onward flight.

Take the private Keisei line (¥260, 10 minutes) or JR (¥200/240 from Terminal 2/1, 10 minutes); Keisei line trains are more frequent. From Tokyo, the easiest way to get to Narita is via the Keisei line from Keisei Ueno Station, taking the Cityliner (¥1790, 41 minutes) or the express (tokkyu; ¥840, 71 minutes). Note that most JR Narita Express trains do not stop at Narita.

From either Narita's JR or Keisei stations, wander down the sinuous

and atmospheric Omote-sandō – an old road that preserves the area's traditional architecture – towards the Buddhist temple of Narita-san Shinshōji. Its landscaped grounds are among the largest in the country – follow a few of its myriad walking paths, but be sure to save time for checking out the Niomon entrance gate, the three-storeyed pagoda and the other impressive temple buildings.

Left: the Buddhist temple of Narita-san Shinshōji as found in central Narita

93

SKIING UP, SNOWBOARDING DOWN

SUNNMØRE ALPS, NORWAY

© River Emilio Thompson. Next page: © Emil Eriksson | 500px

At 1420m (4659ft) up on Blæja peak the silence is total. Far below is the Hjørundfjord, one of the many deep-blue fjords that glisten between rows of snow-capped mountains in Norway's Sunnmøre Alps. It's phenomenal to just be here, but now I'm about to strap in and let gravity take me for a wild ride...

I've snowboarded for much of my life, but this was my first time ski touring and using a splitboard – essentially a pair of cross-country skis that clip together to make a snowboard. The 1000m (3280ft) ascent earlier, from outside the quaint alpine Villa Norangdal guest house, was taken gently. It was a curiously meditative activity, heading up as the April sun formed tiny crystals on the crisp marshmallow snow. With skins on my skis, every gentle slide was a little more suspended gravity earned, and there was ample time to dream about the line I'd take through the untouched powder on my way down.

A few hours later and I'm about to live out that fantasy in full. Boarding downhill is a happy blur of long, gliding turns mixed in with magical glimpses of the fjord below, with the silence disturbed only by my own hooting and hollering. It's a feeling of pure joy and total freedom, and for the rest of the day I can barely stop smiling.

By Toby Skinner

The steep ski ascent has its rich boarding rewards

After the snowy adventures it's to the coast to sleep ↓

The Take Away

Ski touring in Norway was a revelation – it combined the rewarding satisfaction of conquering a peak with the sheer ecstasy of descending down a slope of pristine, velvet-soft powder in the majestic Sunnmøre Alps.

The Build Up

Ski touring in central Norway is best between March and mid-May when the snow conditions are ideal and the days are growing longer. Local experience in the area is crucial, so always head out with a qualified local guide.

Headnorth (headnorth.no), a company run by Englishman Brendan Slater and his Norwegian wife Sissel Tangen, plot tailored itineraries to the wilds of central Norway, most of them combining ski touring with professional guides by day and low-key luxury accommodation by night. Sleep at options such as the old, family-run Hotel Union Øye (unionoye. no) and the gorgeous, modern Juvet Landscape Hotel (juvet.com), which was the main setting for 2014 film *Ex Machina*. The week-long Tafjord and Sunnmøre trip costs €3300 per person. Other companies operate day-long ski tours in the region, including Adrenaline Hunter's (adrenaline-hunter.com) from £364 per person.

Whatever you choose, you'll fly into the pretty Art Nouveau coastal town of Ålesund, where the best place to stay is the chic, waterside Hotel Brosundet (brosundet.no).

Above: skiing down is always an option if you're a die-hard two planker

94

A FREE RIDE

NIZWA TO MUSCAT, OMAN

I was in the city of Nizwa, queuing for a taxi to the capital on the coast some 160km (100 miles) away, when an Arab man in a car drove up and asked, 'Muscat?'

His car was old and a bit beat up, but clean. And he was probably in his mid-twenties. It was at this point that my traveller senses were tingling, reminding me that it's often not wise to get in a car with a stranger and that there is no such thing as a free lunch. But as Oman had so far captivated me at every turn – revealing itself as probably the closest to classical Arabia as you are going to find in the 21st century – I decided to go with the flow and take him up on his offer.

We had as much of a conversation as you can have without knowing each other's language, but we did stop along the way and he purchased some kebabs for us to share. I overcame the problem of telling him the location of my hotel by showing him my iPod Touch, which had the address written in Arabic.

It was just after sunset when we arrived. I quickly dropped my bag in the lobby, but when I turned around to say my goodbyes and to thank him, he was already gone. This stranger had driven me across his country, refused offers of money for fuel and kebabs, and didn't even stick around for a thank you.

By Gary Arndt

The Take Away

This experience totally changed how I view the Arab world. The narrative the media presents, particularly about the region's people, doesn't capture the reality on the ground. Whenever I witness scaremongering now, I recall the man whose name I never got, the one who showed me the goodness of his heart.

The Build Up

Oman is one of the easiest countries on the Arabian Peninsula to visit and explore. English is widely spoken, most signs are in English as well as in Arabic, fuel is cheap and the roads are in excellent condition.

It's an incredibly rewarding country too, offering visitors the rare chance to seek out the modern face of Arabia while still having the ability to absorb its ancient soul. Here, it's possible to engage with the Arab world without the distorting lens of excessive wealth seen elsewhere; low-rise towns are still steeped in their traditional charms and Bedouin values remain at the heart of an Omani welcome. Natural beauty abounds, due to mountains, deserts and a stunning coastline.

Muscat is well connected to Europe, Asia and the Middle East by direct flights. It's also possible to reach the capital by bus or car from Dubai. Visas (required for most nationalities) are available on arrival or online through the Royal Oman Police website (www.rop.gov.om). Regular buses and taxis link Muscat with the historic city of Nizwa.

Left: the road leading to Muscat, the largest city in Oman and its capital
Above: the local kebabs are appetising enough to fuel any journey

95

Last light makes for a quick dash and splash

TWILIGHT SURF

MANGAMAUNU, KAIKOURA, NEW ZEALAND

Below: the surfing at Mangamaunu is said by some to be better after the quake of 2017

It had been a long drive. For weeks I'd trundled my vintage campervan over winding passes and down bumpy dirt tracks in search of surf. But as I followed the twisting coastal road, snow-flecked mountains looming to my left and the iron-grey Pacific stretching endlessly to my right, Mangamaunu finally hove into view.

Arriving at this sweeping, boulder-strewn bay felt like dropping off the edge of the world. In the twilight, land and sea took on a monochrome hue that made it hard to distinguish cliff from beach from ocean. However, there was no mistaking the rhythmic pounding of perfect waves unfurling across the bay, nor the familiar nervous anticipation growing in my gut.

In the dying light my time was short, and as I paddled out, the lone surfer in the water caught a beautiful reeling wave to the beach. I was on my own but for the wildlife teeming all around me: a welcome intruder in an alien landscape, elemental and wonderful.

My wave came and I paddled hard, feeling that familiar drop as its energy took over, the salty spray in my mouth, the sting in my eyes. It curled over me and I screamed in exhilaration, my mind taking a snapshot I'll never forget – an extraordinary panorama framed by the wave's translucent lip encircling me. And then it hit, hurling me under, rolling me over and over until I found myself on my hands and knees on the shore, laughing maniacally in glee and relief.

By Duncan Madden

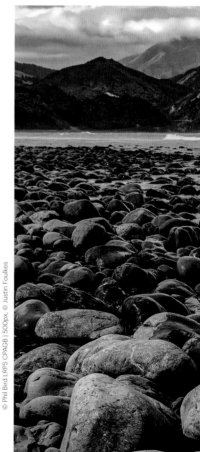

The Take Away

Besides the extraordinary setting and perfect waves, it was the sheer physicality of the experience that I'll never forget. The stupor and fatigue of weeks of unrewarded exploring was obliterated in a heartbeat of unfettered release. I've been surfing for 20 years and it's the most memorable wave I've ever ridden.

The Build Up

Mangamaunu is a few miles north along State Hwy 1 from Kaikoura, a popular town on the east coast of New Zealand's South Island. Its extraordinary setting facing the snow-capped Kaikoura Ranges combined with long, fun waves make it popular with locals and visitors alike.

A right-hand point break, Mangas, as it's known, works best with a northeast-to-easterly swell direction and westerly winds. You can surf it on all tides, but you'll find the smallest crowds and best winds in the early mornings and late afternoons. Although not as powerful as some waves along this coast, it's not a spot for novice surfers.

You can sort wetsuits, surfboards and accommodation in Kaikoura. But for the full experience, Christchurch has lots of van rental companies – among them Classic Campers (classic-campers.com) for the vintage option – and thanks to New Zealand's relaxed attitude it's free for campervans to park and stay at the beach, as long as you clean up after yourself and respect the environment.

96

MOMENT AT MACHU PICCHU

CUZCO REGION, PERU

At the pip of six o'clock, the park entry gates to the 15th-century citadel of the Incas opened and my son and I were almost at the top of the jostling queue. A robust early-morning drenching of rain had cleansed the sky, whisking away the winter mists that rise from the Rio Urubamba way below. The ascending sun was burnishing the shadowed terraces and trails with gauzy light. We agreed to part ways. Following the rush of hard-core hikers, my son would race up to the fabled Sun Gate while I proceeded downwards at a gentler pace.

Nobody followed me as I clutched a much-studied map and descended along stony defiles, past ritual mounds and funerary huts, and edged my way via zigzag steps in a roundabout route. As I sat to catch my breath, a llama appeared, head cocked. I took its picture as it posed, statue-still, as leggy and haughty as a supermodel. It seemed to be standing guard. Neither of us moved. Did it sense I was panicked about my fitness and dodgy balance? No one else had opted for this gentler route and when my son eventually joined me, it clip-clopped away, head held high. But for more than half an hour I had felt completely alone with my llama escort at one of the most-visited wonders of the world. Those extraordinary relics of ancient masonry gleamed as gold as the fabled treasures of the Incas as my heart beat with unbridled joy.

By Susan Kurosawa
Travel Editor, The Weekend Australian

© San Hoyano, © Daniel Neukirch | 500px

The Take Away

After major surgery and ongoing issues with weakening eyesight, I approached Machu Picchu as a terrifying challenge. My balance was unsteady, but a commitment to make this the trip of a lifetime for my son propelled me to tackle what I could, at my own pace. Perhaps no other visitor walked as slowly, but I felt such a sense of achievement. The next afternoon we returned for more, exploring side by side, my pace quickening with every step.

The Build Up

All visitors taking transport to Machu Picchu must pass through Aguas Calientes, a small town that sits in a deep gorge below the ruins. It's only accessible by railway from the rest of the region. Although it's shabby and has a Wild West feel, it offers those who spend the night a distinct leg up on many other Machu Picchu visitors – the chance to gain access to the site first thing in the morning, a time when visitor numbers are at their minimum. Buses trundle up to Machu Picchu between 5.30am to 3.30pm. Alternatively, you can also huff it up the 8km (5 mile) mountain road on foot.

If you really feel like stretching your legs, hike the famed Inca Trail over a course of four or five days to reach Machu Picchu. Permit numbers are strictly limited, but you can book in advance (machupicchu.gob.pe). Other intense but rewarding trekking routes to the historical site include the Lares, Salcantay, Cachicata and Vilcabamba trails.

Entrance tickets (S152) for the morning (6am-noon) and afternoon (noon-5.30pm) sessions often sell out, so get them well in advance via your tour operator, online or in Cuzco.

Left: the incredible Inca citadel of Machu Picchu
Above: llamas inhabit the mountainous areas of Peru

97

SPACE SHUTTLE LAUNCH

TITUSVILLE, FLORIDA, USA

If you're going to sleep in a city park in central Florida, it might as well be the night before the Space Shuttle's final launch. My friend Rob and I had always dreamed of seeing a lift-off, having grown up during the programme's glory days, when astronauts – our heroes – seemed to soar into orbit every month. Finally, in the summer of 2011, the stars suddenly aligned and we drove south toward the Kennedy Space Center with neither a place to stay nor much of a plan beyond being there.

We pulled up near William J Menzo Park in Titusville, not far from Launch Complex 39, and found space for our tent along the scrubby shore. As we joined a few others in pounding stakes into the sandy turf, an atypically cold drizzle started to fall. It was only then we realised that we'd failed to bring much in the way of warm clothing, or a camp stove for that matter. Sometime in the middle of the night inspiration struck to solve the latter and soon a few frosted cherry Pop Tarts were toasting on the engine block of our SUV.

By morning, there were hundreds of people milling around, with almost as many radios crackling with 'T-minus' updates. Our ad hoc community shared stories of past triumphs – the launches seen, the missions accomplished – and the tragedies too. As Atlantis took off, booming into the heavens, the crowd let out huge cheers, tinged with melancholy about an uncertain future for human exploration.

By Paul Brady
Articles Editor, Condé Nast Traveler

The Take Away

Although I grew up loving model rockets, Isaac Asimov stories and *Star Trek*, nothing compared to the excitement of seeing an actual spaceship blast into orbit on a rail of fire and smoke. Yet, I couldn't forget that it also marked the end of an era, one that sparked pride and optimism in an entire generation of Americans.

The Take Away

The Space Shuttle may have stopped flying these days but it is still possible to watch rockets depart Planet Earth. Both cargo and military launches continue along Florida's Space Coast at Cape Canaveral – from where the Mercury and Gemini missions were launched – and you can watch Elon Musk's SpaceX programme in action at the Kennedy Space Center. A full list of upcoming launches is available to view at wearegofl.com/launches.

The only place to regularly see manned flights today is the Baikonur Cosmodrome in Kazakhstan, from which crews travel to the International Space Station. Although the place is steeped in Space Race and Cold War history, getting there and actually witnessing a launch is famously difficult as it remains under Russian control. Your best bet is to employ the services of a specialist tour operator such as Vegitel (starcity-tours.com), which reportedly has close ties to Roscosmos and can handle all the logistics and permits.

In China, the Jiuquan Satellite Launch Center has also launched manned trips to orbit, but no future trips are scheduled until at least 2019. Wenchang Spacecraft Launch Site on Hainan Island may – someday – support a Chinese crew's mission to the moon, but no need to book just yet as that trip won't likely happen until at least 2036.

Above: crowds watch the Space Shuttle Atlantis blast off from central Florida on 8 July 2011
Left: campers looking towards Launch Complex 39

MEETING THE NAGA BABAS

HARIDWAR, INDIA

Naked, often coated in ash and occasionally draped with flowers, the dreadlocked naga babas (or naga sadhus as they are also known) are Hinduism's fiercest ascetics – they have renounced almost everything we can imagine.

Having gathered in the thousands for Kumbh Mela in Haridwar, the nagas were front and centre for most of the festivities. Late one night I came upon a group of them camped out around their ceremonial fire pits on the bank of the River Ganges. Fascinated, I waded into their midst. Sitting and chatting, I made fast friends with Maharaj Phiri Giri Baba – we talked of life and India, the country we both grew up in. When the time came to make my way, he sucked deeply on his hash pipe and asked for my address. I instinctively handed him my business card from my marketing job at Google. Glancing at it, he said something that both amazed and delighted me. He'd never used a computer, had little knowledge of the English language and had dropped out of school in his youth to pursue an ascetic lifestyle, yet he looked up and said in Hindi: 'Oh, yes, Google, very powerful website.'

On my way back to my camp, I was surprised again by another naga baba who had a mobile phone to his ear and was talking excitedly, finger stabbing the air. Obviously he hadn't renounced his phone! It's the paradoxes of modern India that truly confound and excite.

By Gopi Kallayil

The Take Away

Perhaps this experience explains why Indian civilisation has survived for millennia – it has one foot firmly rooted in its past, while the other's toes test the quicksand of an uncertain but exciting future. And maybe that's why I embrace my heritage, but love innovation and thrive on the expansion that travel brings.

The Build Up

Haridwar, the holiest Hindu city in the state of Uttarakhand, is auspiciously situated where the River Ganges emerges from the Himalayas. It's here at Har-ki-Pairi Ghat, next to the fast-flowing river, where Vishnu – the second god in the Hindu triumvirate – is said to have dropped some divine nectar and left behind a footprint. As such, the site attracts pilgrims by the droves, but none more so than when it hosts Kumbh Mela every 12 years. During this festival countless millions flood into the city.

The city is also particularly busy during the *yatra* (pilgrimage) season that runs annually from May to October. Things tend to reach a peak each July when Shiva devotees, numbering in the hundreds of thousands, make their way to the city. Haridwar is well connected by bus and rail services to Delhi, although it's always advisable to make reservations early during *yatra*.

The next Kumbh Mela in Haridwar takes place in 2022, though encountering naga babas is possible across India throughout the year, particularly at Hindu festivals and in the Himalayan regions.

Left: the naga babas renounce materialism and take a vow of celibacy

99

RIDING THE ROAD OF BONES

NIZHNY BESTYAKH TO MAGADAN, RUSSIA

Charley and Ewan, motors running on the Kolyma Hwy

Few roads are paved with the skeletons of those who built it, but the Kolyma Hwy is certainly no ordinary road. And my trip along it with Ewan McGregor, as part of our documentary series Long Way Round, changed my life and his.

At the start of our journey we were green to the world of adventure travel. We didn't know what to expect or how things would turn out, but we had one big challenge – to ride our motorcycles along the 'road of bones' through eastern Russia. And my word, it certainly challenged us (more than I could have possibly imagined). Due to permafrost under its length, the road becomes a bog with endless river crossings during summer, and we had to dig ramps to get into (and out of) many of them. Then there were the huge sinkholes we needed to fill with salvaged wood... it went on and on. And on.

I remember our first night. We had ridden for 14 hours when an eerie dusk settled, and I started to think about all the terrible things that happened there. Sleeping on the road itself, above the bones of those who'd suffered the worst possible pain and fate, was our only option given the marshy roadsides. Although Ewan and I were there together, it imparted such a sense of loneliness.

Extraordinarily difficult and full of high emotions, the journey was also profoundly rewarding – it not only changed our lives but our perceptions of travel and adventure.

By Charley Boorman

© Charley Boorman

A roadside break on a life-changing Russian adventure

The Take Away

No matter what challenge or destination lies ahead of me now, I never feel daunted. This journey showed me how much I'm capable of, and just how far I can push myself. It also taught me that most people around the world are good, welcoming and want to help you.

The Build Up

Needless to say, the notorious Kolyma Hwy (aka the 'road of bones') is a challenge for the most toughened adventurers. It's not known how many Gulag labourers froze to death building it, but the permafrost conditions meant corpses were buried in the road instead of next to it.

From the remote city of Yakutsk, the 'road of bones' makes for an incredibly tough 2200km (1370 mile) journey east to Magadan on the Sea of Okhotsk. Along the way you'll see the Verkhoyansk Mountains, visit Oymyakon (holding the unique title of 'the world's coldest inhabited town'), pass a few former Gulag camps, take in the ghost mining town of Kadykchan and cross (as Charley attests) countless rivers.

Besides tackling the road with an all-terrain motorcycle, options to travel along it include negotiating a ride with a truck, hiring a 6WD vehicle or contacting Visit Yakutia (visityakutia.com), which is a specialist tour operator that covers the route. It leads 10-day group tours in both summer and winter, and also offers some self-drive packages (costs vary widely depending on the size of the group and numerous other factors).

Below: in keeping with its grim history, the 'road of bones' presents many obstacles along its route

MAKING A CONNECTION

YAZD, IRAN

Dusk was falling as I entered the market, a warren of covered, arched corridors filled with tempting piles of products: a clatter of silver tea sets stacked here, an unsteady arrangement of copper pans there, a veritable Ali Baba's cave of dishes, clothing, crafts and spices...

As I headed outside I was too absorbed by the tumbling arrays of colourful fruit and vegetables, and exotic, unfamiliar sights, such as a display of decapitated goat heads, to notice that my companions and I were slowly being surrounded. But the feeling was far from menacing. As I looked up, shoppers – families with small children, pairs of friends, old women with reluctant husbands – were smiling and saying hello, first shyly, then, as we smiled back, with

more confidence, asking us what we were doing there and thanking us for visiting their country.

Iran has always been portrayed in the media with such an air of suspicion, so it was heartwarming to mix with its people, who badly wanted to make it known that they were just like us, and worthy of our focus.

'What do you like most about Iran?' was asked a dozen times. 'You,' I replied, tears forming, 'the people. You make us feel so welcome.' I felt shame that we often don't do the same in the West. But I felt gladdened beyond words that these residents of the planet, who live under the same sun, with the same blood running through their veins, only wanted to connect.

By Laura Millar

The Take Away

At a time when there has never been more mistrust between East and West, it was striking, and humbling, to realise that we are all connected by our sheer, basic humanity. I may not share their culture, religion or history, but our basic impulses joined us; the impulse to connect with, and understand, our fellow man.

The Build Up

Valid Iranian visas are required by most nationalities. Acquiring one upon on arrival is possible for people from some countries

(the USA, UK and Canada are not among them), but as the process is fraught with issues many people are turned away. To be safe, get a visa before travelling, and start the process at least two months before you plan to arrive.

Assuming you have a visa, most immigration and border officials are efficient and tourists rarely get too much hassle. Land borders can take longer if you're on a bus or train. Women need to be adequately covered from the moment they get off the plane or arrive at the border.

Contrary to popular misconception, US, UK and

Canadian citizens are welcome, but need to pre-arrange a tour or private guide, or be sponsored by a friend or relative in Iran, who will take legal responsibility for them.

For those that can, travelling independently in Iran has more ups than downs. Air, rail and bus transport is efficient and safe, sights are cheap and enough people speak English, or are willing to help, that it's hard to get into too much trouble.

Left: *shoppers browse stalls under the arches at an Iranian bazaar*

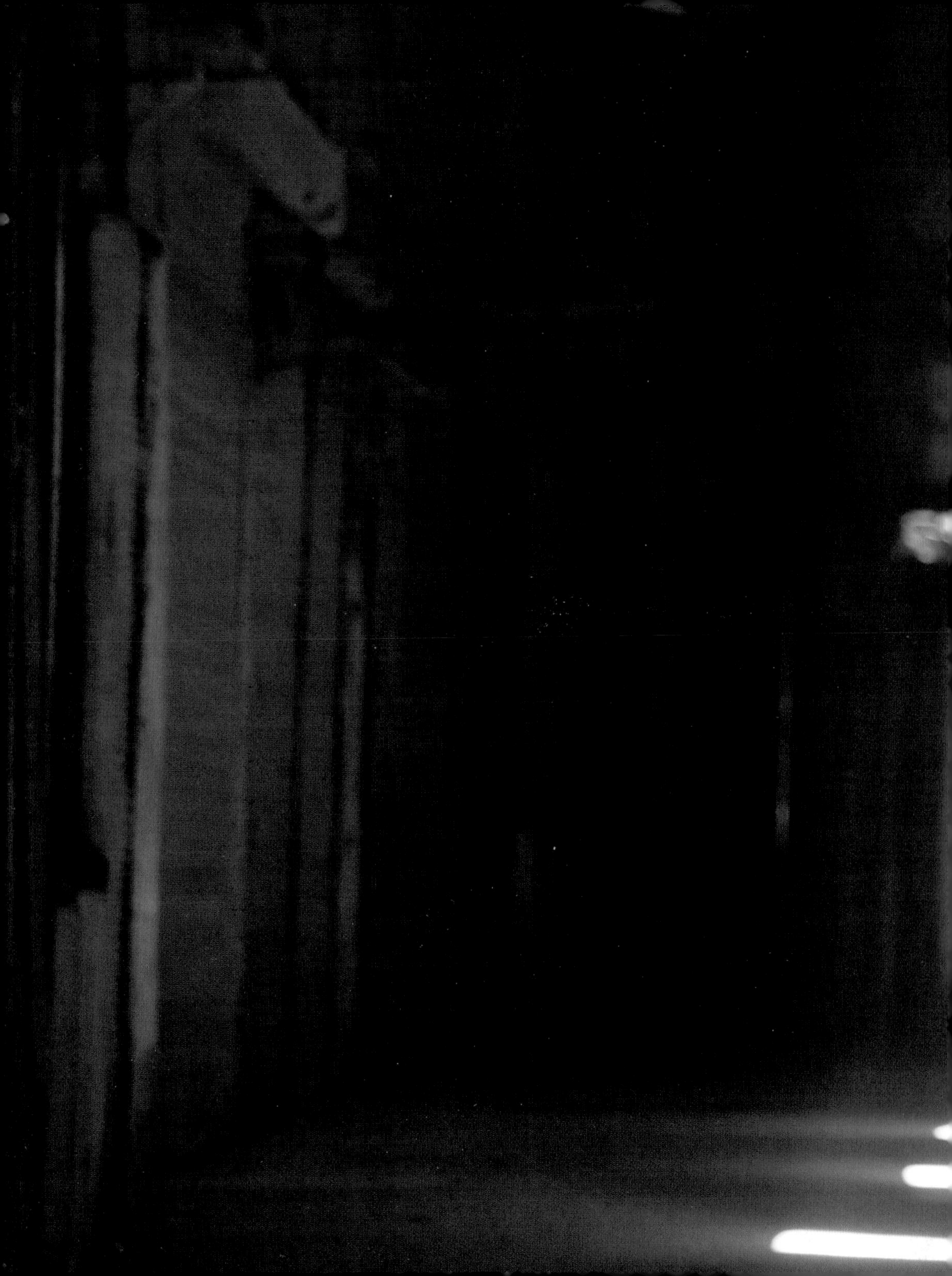

DESTINATION INDEX

A
Afganistan 44
Albania 80
Algeria 80
Antarctica 34, 162
Atlanic Ocean 160
Argentina 228
Australia 55, 70, 154, 216
Austria 15

B
Bosnia 80
Botswana 116
Brazil 28, 236

C
Cambodia 114
Canada 15, 136
Chile 56, 194
China 32, 42, 140, 170, 192, 226, 253
Colombia 124
Croatia 80
Cyprus 80

D
Djibouti 146
Democratic Republic of Congo 63

E
Ecuador 188
Egypt 12, 80
England 96, 183, 218

F
Fiji 50
Finland 15, 202
France 18, 36, 80, 190, 198

G
Gibraltar 80
Greece 80
Greenland 86, 142, 200
Guyana 52, 230

I
Iceland 120, 178
India 8, 24, 92, 130, 174, 208, 212, 256
Indonesia 55
Iran 132, 260
Israel & Palestinian Territories 26, 80
Italy 18, 80

J
Japan 64, 94, 112, 220, 240
Jordan 80, 106

K
Kyrgyzstan 74

L
Laos 164
Libya 80
Lebanon 80

M
Madagascar 126
Mali 185
Mexico 84
Monaco 80
Mongolia 156
Morocco 80, 134
Myanmar 66

N
Namibia 184
Nepal 104
Netherlands 15
New Zealand 248
Norway 242

O
Oman 76, 246

P
Papua New Guinea 54
Peru 166, 250

K
Kazakstan 253

Kenya 40

R
Russia 32, 200, 202, 258
Rwanda 62

S
Saudia Arabia 77
Scotland 183, 222
Slovenia 80
South Africa 22, 152
Spain 36, 80, 150, 206
Sudan 90
Sweden 14
Switzerland 18
Syria 80

T
Tahiti 82
Tanzania 110
Thailand 164
Tibet 42, 140, 174, 226
Tristan da Cunha 152
Tunisa 80
Turkey 80

U
UK 96, 182, 218, 222
Uganda 62, 232
United Arab Emirates 77
USA 15, 16, 46, 60, 72, 122, 144, 172, 252
Uzbekistan 100

V
Vietnam 180

W
Wales 182

Y
Yemen 77, 238

Z
Zambia 102

WRITER BIOS

Dayna Aamodt has had many special moments while travelling, including riding gondolas in Venice, walking with her husband along the Seine in Paris, visiting the Great Wall of China and indulging in pastries in the cafes of Vienna, but nothing compares to the West Coast Trail.

Benedict Allen is one of the world's leading adventurer-explorers. Despite travelling in the modern era, he famously forgoes the technological safety net, choosing to travel without a GPS or phone of any kind. Instead he relies on training and the forging of relationships with the indigenous people he encounters. He has also pioneered the recording of extreme journeys for television.

Will Allen has lived in three cities and travelled to more than a dozen countries across three continents, which in his opinion is not nearly enough.

Gary Arndt is an awarding-winning blogger and travel photographer who has been roving the world since 2007. To date he has visited over 120 countries and more than 335 Unesco World Heritage sites.

Brett Atkinson has travelled to almost 80 countries, and is most content when discovering local flavours or checking out a region's craft beer scene. His favourite international cities are Istanbul, San Francisco and Hanoi. Home is New Zealand.

Amy Balfour has hiked, biked and paddled her way across the United States. Her favourite spots for US-based adventure include the Grand Canyon, the Gauley River, Half Dome and the Racetrack Playa. She has written or co-written more than 30 books for Lonely Planet.

Duff Battye has sheared sheep, bobsleighed, fished, dived with sharks, trekked, skydived, sailed and more while visiting countries as varied as Australia, China, Egypt, Iceland, India, Kiribati, New Zealand, Mexico and Russia. His favourite destination remains North Wales.

Antonia Bolingbroke-Kent is a travel writer, freelance TV producer and director of Edge Expeditions. She has written three books, the latest being *Land of the Dawn-Lit Mountains: A Journey Across Arunachal Pradesh – India's Forgotten Frontier*. Learn more at itinerant.co.uk or follow her on Twitter and Instagram (@AntsBK).

Oliver Berry has had lots of wonderful wildlife encounters, from watching bears in the Rocky Mountains and orang-utans in the Bornean rainforest to swimming with humpback whales in Tonga. His latest adventures are published at oliverberry.com.

Abigail Butcher, inspired by her life's best moment, left a stressful news editor desk job in London to live by the sea in the New Forest, Hampshire, UK. She now travels the world as a freelance adventure travel and ski journalist. Wherever and whenever possible she shares her forays with Thala, her Rhodesian ridgeback and partner in crime.

Claire Beyer is a keen off-the-beaten-track explorer who has also volunteered numerous times with various environmental organisations in Southeast Asia that work in the area of elephant conservation.

Paul Bloomfield is a writer and photographer who's hiked in six continents, tackling trails in India, Morocco and Australia. As well as contributing to Lonely Planet books, he writes for he writes for newspapers and magazines including *The Telegraph*, *Times*, *Independent* and *Wanderlust*.

Cristian Bonetto spends much of his time traversing the globe as a travel writer in search of curious characters, cultural quirks and decent cups of coffee. His main stomping grounds include Los Angeles, New York, Italy, Denmark and his beloved Australia.

Charley Boorman is an actor, travel adventurer and motorcycle enthusiast. His first big adventure was the iconic, award-winning series *Long Way Round*, which saw him and close friend Ewan McGregor motorcycle around the world.

Nick Boulos fell in love with travelling aged four on a trip to Egypt, sparking an affair that continues to this day. As an award-winning travel writer, he has visited more than 100 countries for titles such as the *Washington Post* and *The Sunday Times*.

Paul Brady is articles editor at *Condé Nast Traveler* in New York City. He's written about expats in Mérida, great Riesling in the Finger Lakes and a very strange puppet show in Providence, Rhode Island.

Laura Brown has travelled extensively across the Western Hemisphere, with a particular fondness for photographing

America's National Parks and hiking to watch sunsets from high peaks.

Jean-Bernard Carillet is a Paris-based writer and photographer who specialises in Africa, France, Turkey, the Indian Ocean, the Caribbean and the Pacific. He loves adventure, remote places, outdoors, archaeological sites, food and – unsurprisingly – islands.

Penny Carroll got her first taste of wanderlust in 1992 when her family took an epic, nine-month road trip around Australia. She's been exploring ever since, and now writes for Lonely Planet. Watching the northern lights in Iceland and hiking Tasmania's Overland Track in 3m-deep snow are among her most thrilling travel experiences.

Paul Clammer has worked as a molecular biologist, tour leader and travel writer. Since 2003 he has contributed to around 30 Lonely Planet guides, covering swathes of South and Central Asia, West and North Africa and the Caribbean.

Lucy Corne is a freelance travel and beer writer living in Cape Town. She has travelled to 50 countries and visited every continent bar Antarctica, but Tristan da Cunha remains her proudest passport stamp.

Ruth Cosgrove caught the travel bug when her Mum took her backpacking through Europe at the age of six. Since then she's sailed, walked and written in as many places as possible and plans to keep going.

Duncan Craig is Assistant Travel Editor of *The Sunday Times*, a former *Lonely Planet* magazine features editor, and has twice been shortlisted for AITO Travel Writer of the Year. Specialising in active and adventure travel, he's kayaked in Antarctica, trekked through the Congo and run ultramarathons in the Sahara.

Sophie Cunningham has been travelling since 1982, which is about five years longer than she's been working in publishing and as a writer. She's the author of four books. Her main ports of call have been India, Indonesia and the United States but she's hoping to expand her repertoire.

Fionn Davenport has been a travel writer since the mid-1990s (around the time he trekked Tiger Leaping Gorge; p. 192) and, despite travelling the world in pursuit of a good travel story, has yet to make it back to China.

Liz Edwards didn't board a plane or eat a curry till she was 17; she's been catching up ever since, visiting 50-plus countries to write about travel, food, or both. She's currently associate editor of *The Sunday Times Travel Magazine.*

Mark Eveleigh almost fell into travel writing – he was inspired to start by a nerve-wracking six hours spent dangling on a frayed wire in Venezuelan cable car. Since then he's contributed to 80 international publications. Though based in SE Asia, he's always hankering to get back to Africa. Read more at markeveleigh.com.

Ashley Garver believes travel is one of the most empowering tools to get to know yourself, each other and the world around you. In 2013 she took a year-long sabbatical, traveling solo throughout Southeast Asia, India and Europe.

Ethan Gelber has been travelling well outside of his comfort zone for nearly 30 years, often by bicycle. In 1997, he successfully led an 'educational Internet adventure' team of five cyclists on BikeAbout–the Mediterranean (bikeabout.org).

Don George is the author of *The Way of Wanderlust* and *How to Be a Travel Writer*. He has been a travel writer and editor for the *San Francisco Examiner-Chronicle*, Salon.com, Lonely Planet, and *National Geographic Traveler*. In 40 years he has visited 90 countries on six continents.

John Gimlette is the author of five travel books, and has won the Shiva Naipaul Prize for travel writing, and the Dolman Travel Book Prize for 2012. He lives in London.

David Gorvett has travelled through much of the Americas, Europe and Asia-Pacific and his trip to Tanzania was the tantalizing first of many to come (he hopes) to Africa.

Sally Gray is a writer, editor and primary education specialist. Having edited the Kenya Airways inflight magazine, Africa remains her favourite destination, but her travels have taken her all over the world – from Alaska to New Zealand.

William Gray's time on Heron Island nurtured a fledgling dream to become a photographer and writer. Nearly 30 years later, he's one of the UK's most respected travel journalists with numerous awards to his name,

including AITO Travel Writer of the Year.

Emma Gregg is an award-winning travel journalist who has visited over 30 African countries, sampling everything from obscure music festivals to five-star safaris. Based in the UK, she focuses on responsible tourism, wildlife, nature and culture and is always planning the next adventure.

Anthony Ham writes for magazines and newspapers around the world, and has written more than 120 guidebooks for Lonely Planet. He spent ten years living in Madrid and is most often found travelling in Africa, the Arctic or remote corners of Australia.

Damian Harper, holder of two degrees (History of Art from Leeds University, Modern and Classical Chinese from SOAS), travels the world as a writer for Lonely Planet. His rules: go everywhere with an open mind, prepare to be amazed by what you see and tell everyone about it.

Simon Heptinstall was described as 'a miserable little squirt' by *Private Eye* shortly after he took up journalism (he was formerly a taxi driver and garage manager). He says he's grown a bit and cheered up slightly since then, so only the 'squirt' still applies.

Nicky Holford is equally at home sleeping under the stars in the Wadi Rum desert, dancing to reggae in Jamaica or galloping a horse across the savannah in Botswana. She lives with her husband, Norfolk terrier and horse in the Cotswolds.

Anne Howard quit her job in 2012 as an executive editor in NYC to travel the world with her husband Mike. Considered to be on the world's longest honeymoon, the Howards are leading couples travel experts, sharing their tips on Twitter (@HoneyTrek) and in National Geographic's *Ultimate Journeys for Two.*

Mike Howard has been traveling around the world with his wife Anne ever since they left on their honeymoon in 2012. They've been chronicling their adventures across seven continents and 50+ countries HoneyTrek. com and their National Geographic book, *Ultimate Journeys for Two.*

Aurelia India Birwood made her first trip to Africa in 1997, which was an exciting foray into the streets of Cairo and the Pyramids of Giza. Since then she's returned often, falling for different things each and every visit.

Anita Isalska is a freelance travel writer. Though non-religious, Anita's travels have taken her to pilgrimage sites from Lourdes in France to Bulgaria's Rila Monastery. Anita covered Jerusalem for Lonely Planet's latest *Israel & the Palestinian Territories* guide.

Pico Iyer is the author of many books on the travel shelves, including *Video Night in Kathmandu*, *The Lady and the Monk* and, most recently, *The Man Within My Head* and *The Open Road.*

Brian Jackman is Britain's foremost writer on wildlife safaris. He's also a journalist and author (with Jonathan Scott) of *The Marsh Lions*. He is a patron of Tusk Trust and a trustee of the George Adamson Wildlife Preservation Trust.

Suzanne Joinson is an award winning novelist, her books *A Lady Cyclist's Guide to Kashgar* and *The Photographer's Wife* are published by Bloomsbury. She regularly writes for the *New York Times* and other publications.

Wailana Kalama is a freelance travel writer from Hawaii, but currently hanging her hat in Stockholm. She's travelled through 40 countries, and lived in six. She has a complicated relationship with jet lag.

Gopi Kallayil pored over travel books about the world beyond his native India while growing up. Today he's travelled through nearly 60 countries and all seven continents – he is more awed than ever at the huge, diverse world we occupy.

Susan Kurosawa first travelled, at age seven, with her foreign correspondent father from England to France, where he insisted she learn "the art of observation". Based in Sydney, she has written eight books, including a best-selling novel, and has been Travel Editor of *The Weekend Australian* since 1992.

Jamie Lafferty is a Scottish travel writer and photographer who has visited over 100 countries and Antarctica three times (so far). He hates the smell of penguin guano, right up until he can't smell it any more. Read more at jamielafferty.com.

Robert Landon has lived a block from Copacabana beach for six years and has co-authored two editions of Lonely Planet's *Brazil* guide. He has attended Carnival as both a single and married, man. Both are magical, but if you can choose, he recommends the former.

Chris Leadbeater is a British travel journalist who has been filling his passport with niche stamps (many of them South American) for 20 years. He lives in London, but is working his way towards the feted 100-country mark (and has now reached 85), so is rarely ever there.

John Lee has been a full-time travel writer for 20 years, specialising in stories on beer, cities and trains. He has been a Lonely Planet contributor, concentrating on Vancouver and British Columbia, since 2005. Track his travels at johnleewriter.com.

Stephen Lioy is a photographer and travel writer based in the Central Asian state of Kyrgyzstan, where he's equally likely to be found in the hipster cafes of Bishkek or wild mountains of the Tien.

Ian MacEacheran was the first Scotsman to climb the North Face of the Eiger in Switzerland and has summited peaks in the Alps, Andes and Rockies. He has travelled from Costa Rica to Kenya, meeting gorillas in Uganda and coatis in Brazil along the way, yet is still happiest when in the mountains.

Mike MacEachearan is an Edinburgh-based writer and author who regularly contributes to *Lonely Planet* magazine, as well as to *The Guardian, The Sunday Times, Condé Nast Traveller* and BBC. In his search for the ultimate travel moment, he has visited 107 countries.

Duncan Madden has spent twenty years dragging body and board along the world's coastlines in search of empty waves, natural wonders and the perpetual sensation of being on holiday. He's told these stories in magazines, newspapers, travel guides and books.

James Gabriel Martin is a photojournalist with a passion for documenting the rich culture and stunning scenery in each of the places that he travels.

Andrew McCarthy is author of the *New York Times* best selling travel memoir *The Longest Way Home* and the young adult novel *Just Fly Away*. He is an editor at large for *National Geographic Traveler*. He is also an actor and director.

Daniel McCrohan is a UK-born, Asia-travel specialist who has been backpacking his way around the world for 25 years. He's worked on more than 30 guidebooks – for both Lonely Planet and Trailblazer – and posts off-the-beaten-track videos on danielmccrohan.com.

Richard Mellor, a former PR executive for travel companies, realised that he preferred writing about foreign lands rather than showing them to visiting journalists. Based in London, he specialises in Europe and cities, and loves nature, obscure historical titbits and anything newfangled or strange.

Aaron Millar is an award-winning journalist, author and the 2014 British Guild of Travel Writer's Travel Writer of the Year. Originally from Brighton, England he now hides out in the Rocky Mountains of Colorado. Read more at thebluedotperspective.com; @AaronMWriter

Laura Millar is an award-winning, London-based travel writer who grew up in Scotland. Having travelled to only France for the first sixteen years of her life (thanks to her French mother), she developed an insatiable wanderlust which has taken her to countries like Haiti, Iran, Patagonia and Lebanon.

Korina Miller grew up on Vancouver Island and has been exploring the globe independently since she was the age of 16, visiting or living in 36 countries and working with cultural organisations and minority groups. She has written nearly 40 titles for Lonely Planet.

Thomas Mills has logged many hours on Vancouver's ultimate fields and his Frisbee skills have come in handy on many adventurous journeys throughout the world, whether in Timbuktu, Katmandu, Bahir Dar, the Yukon or Hanoi.

Joe Minihane has travelled across Asia from Japan to Myanmar, tracked wild dogs in the Kenyan bush and eaten his way around New York's Outer Boroughs. He's happiest finding new wild swimming spots in his native UK.

Katharine Nelson dates her love of travel to a solo trip around South America when she was 18. She's followed this passion around the world since, hitting a particular high in Japan. Originally from Brighton, she now lives in London and works in marketing for Lonely Planet.

Sarah Outen MBE is an adventurer by land and sea. She has spent over a year, cumulatively, rowing solo across the world's oceans. Author of two books and a motivational speaker, she is an advocate of time spent outdoors, whether doing, being or exploring.

Simon Parker is a travel writer and foreign correspondent that has reported from almost 100 countries. He makes TV and radio documentaries from all over the world and specialises in adventure travel. In 2016 he sailed and cycled from China to London, travelling east via the North Pacific.

Stephanie Pearson is a contributing editor to *Outside* magazine. She has meditated in Bhutan, dogsledded in Arctic Sweden, and circumnavigated Lake Superior, among many other fun adventures. She is yet to be fully enlightened and lives in northern Minnesota.

Stephen Phelan is an Irish writer who developed a wanderlust through the tall tales of his sailor father. He has lived in Scotland, Australia, Japan and Argentina but is now settled in Madrid with his adopted street dog from Buenos Aires.

Adrian Phillips is Managing Director of Bradt Travel Guides, and an award-winning travel writer and broadcaster who has written feature articles on everything from swamp-walking in the Everglades to seafood safaris in Sweden.

Matt Phillips was a Vancouver-based geologist working in gold mines of northern British Columbia when travel changed his life. After stints writing and researching Lonely Planet guides to countries across North America, Asia and Africa, he became editor of UK-based *Travel Africa* magazine. In 2013 he returned to Lonely Planet to become Destination Editor to sub-Saharan Africa. Home is happily now on the bank of the Thames in Hammersmith, London.

Jane Powell grew up in England before moving to Canada with her family while in her teens. A career in teaching followed and allowed her the time to notch up some rather memorable travel experiences across the globe, ranging from Australia to Venezuela.

Lori Rackl, driven by FOMO (fear of missing out) and wanderlust, has travelled to more than 70 countries, many of which she visited while backpacking through Europe in the early '90s. She's now the Travel Editor of the *Chicago Tribune*.

Sarah Reid is a former Destination Editor at Lonely Planet. She is now a globetrotting freelance travel writer for some of the world's top travel publishers. She also blogs about all things sustainable travel-related at ecotravelist.com.

Kait Reynolds is a writer and designer from Austin, Texas. Recently she traded her suit for a plane ticket, and has been exploring the world without an end in sight. Find out more at kaitflaked.com.

Brendan Sainsbury, when not competing in dubiously-inspired endurance events, has contributed to over 50 Lonely Planet guidebooks with a strong preference for Cuba, Spain and Alaska.

Toby Skinner is a freelance editor and travel writer, who was formerly editorial development director at Ink, the world's biggest travel media company. He likes meeting local characters, sea swimming and adventures in cold places.

Oliver Smith is a features writer for *Lonely Planet* magazine, and a devotee of deserts from the Atacama to the Sahara. He was named Travel Writer of the Year 2017 at the Travel Media Awards.

Phoebe Smith is an award-winning editor, travel writer, author and presenter. By night she's an extreme sleeping outdoors adventurer who thrives on finding the strangest places to sleep in wild locations.

Paul Stiles began writing for Lonely Planet soon after seeing 'the Shadow' atop El Teide in Tenerife (p. 150). He has subsequently covered Morocco, Madagascar, Borneo, the Philippines, São Tomé and Príncipe, Nepal, and most of the Hawaiian Islands. He still lives in Spain.

Mark Stratton is a writer, photographer, and radio broadcaster based in the wilds of Dartmoor National Park. He has a preference for any journey that steps outside his comfort zone and for adventures to places most people have never heard of.

Hannah Summers is a writer whose career was born out of her love of two things: burgers and Bruce Springsteen. When she's not following Bruce around the world, you're likely to find her drinking in a backstreet bar or munching some unidentifiable street food (with The Boss on her headphones, of course).

Jurriaan Teulings is an award-winning, serendipity-driven travel writer and photographer. He has covered all continents and comfort zones, from Amazonian *ayahuasca* communes and Iranian underground parties to cross-continental luxury trains and private islands. Home is Amsterdam.

Katalin Thomann has travelled extensively, volunteering in Tibet, Cambodia, Sri Lanka and Iran while working for organisations such as Amnesty International. She has surfed in the Maldives, kayaked in Alaska and snowboarded in Uzbekistan, but is equally at home in Edinburgh where she lives.

Emma Thomson is an award-winning freelance travel writer that spends roughly three quarters of the year on the road searching out stories – the more adventurous the better. Assignments have ranged from camping wild on the Antarctic Peninsula and walking the length of Namibia's Skeleton Coast to travelling the length of the ancient Silk Road.

Jonathan Thompson is a recent British Travel Writer of the Year, and is a regular contributor to publications including *The Daily Telegraph*, *The Sunday Times*, *The Guardian*, *Men's Health* and *Condé Nast Traveller*. Now based in Dallas, Texas, he specialises in US travel and has visited all 50 states.

Marcel Theroux is an award-winning novelist and broadcaster who writes regularly for *Lonely Planet* magazine. His novels include *Far North* and *Strange Bodies*, and most recently, *The Secret Books*.

Nigel Tisdall is an award-winning British travel writer and photographer whose globetrotting career began one wet Monday morning in 1985 when he went to London's Liverpool Street station and caught a train to Hong Kong. Since then he's roamed all over the world writing for leading newspapers and magazines including *The Telegraph* and *Financial Times*.

Hugo Turner is a British adventurer from Devon. Since the age of 17, when he broke his neck in a near catastrophic diving accident, he has been accomplishing goals – along with his twin brother – that no one else has ever achieved, all in aid of the spinal cord research. More details at theturnertwins.co.uk

Ross Turner has rowed across the Atlantic, climbed Mount Elbrus and trekked across the polar ice caps of Greenland, all with his identical twin brother Hugo. Most recently the Turner Twins have become the first adventurers to reach the Australian and South American poles of inaccessibility. Find out more at theturnertwins.co.uk.

Nicola Trup is a London-based freelance travel journalist and editor. Formerly Deputy Head of Travel for *The Independent* and the *London Evening Standard*, she's a fan of big landscapes, spicy food and classic Americana.

Mike Unwin has travelled much of the world searching for wildlife and writes regularly about his experiences for *The Telegraph*, *The Independent*, *BBC Wildlife* and other publications. A specialist in Africa, his many books include the *Bradt Guide to Southern African Wildlife*.

Neil Wilson fled the rat race of the oil industry only four years after graduating as a geologist and has travelled and climbed in four continents. He has written more than 80 travel guidebooks for a range of publishers.

Georgina Wilson-Powell has been an editor for 15 years and a travel journalist for eight. She's lived in Dubai, France, Ireland and Australia, is obsessed with New Nordic food, loves an American roadtrip and is currently exploring the country on her doorstep, the UK.

Tasmin Waby is a writer and editor who grew up in Melbourne, Australia. Her latest adventures see her living on a narrowboat on Regent's Canal in London, a city she's called home on and off her whole life. She still loves night time – and snow.

Tony Wheeler made a trek along the Hippie Trail in 1972 that led him to write the very first Lonely Planet guide and left him with a lifetime travel addiction. Recently Tony travelled back across Asia in the opposite direction along the Silk Road.

Art Wolfe is an award-winning photographer who has worked on every continent. His photographs of indigenous cultures, vast landscapes, and wildlife are recognised for their mastery of colour, composition, and perspective. He has published over 100 books, including his magnum opus *Earth Is My Witness*, and is the host of the television series *Art Wolfe's Travels to the Edge*. Read more at artwolfe.com.

Chris Zeiher describes himself as a massive Scandi-file, a Eurovision-tragic and wannabe wine connoisseur. His travels have taken him around the globe, from discovering boutique wine regions in Tasmania and enjoying delicious treats on the streets of Tokyo to escaping hippos on the Chobe River in Botswana and stumbling across lava fields in Iceland.

ACKNOWLEDGEMENTS

Published in September 2018
by Lonely Planet Global Limited
CRN 554153
www.lonelyplanet.com
ISBN 978 17870 1357 5
© Lonely Planet 2018
Printed in Singapore
10 9 8 7 6 5 4 3 2 1

Managing Director, Publishing Piers Pickard
Associate Publisher Robin Barton
Commissioning Editor & Editor Matt Phillips
Proofing Nick Mee
Art Direction Daniel Di Paolo
Layout & Image Research Tina García
Print Production Nigel Longuet

Thanks to Neill Coen, Flora Macqueen, Tasmin Waby

STAY IN TOUCH lonelyplanet.com/contact

AUSTRALIA
The Malt Store, Level 3, 551 Swanston St,
Carlton, Victoria 3053 T: 03 8379 8000

USA
124 Linden St, Oakland, CA 94607
T: 510 250 6400

IRELAND
Digital Depot, Roe Lane (off Thomas St), Digital Hub,
Dublin 8, D08 TCV4

UNITED KINGDOM
240 Blackfriars Rd, London SE1 8NW
T: 020 3771 5100